RAINER MARIA RILKE is one of the finest poets of our
century, and without a doubt the greatest German
poet since Goethe. Sixty years after his death in 1926
his influence is ever growing, capturing the hearts
and imagination of an ever wider readership, especially in the English-speaking world. The intimate,
intense and lyrical voice of Rilke speaks directly to
the concerns and yearnings of men and women
today.

Albert Flemming's acclaimed translations represent
the fruition of a lifetime's reading and reflection on
Rilke's poetry from which he has sought both inspiration and a spiritual comfort.

This is the most comprehensively representative
single selection of Rilke's verse in English. Here are
over 120 poems from his nine most important collections of verse, including the *Duino Elegies,* the
crowning expression of his poetic vision. A number
of these poems have never previously been translated into English.

This volume of wonderfully resonant and faithful
translations constitute the ideal introduction to
Rilke's verse for those coming to it for the first time.
For those already familiar with Rilke's poetry,
Flemming will reveal it anew.

RAINER MARIA
RILKE

SELECTED POEMS

TRANSLATED BY

Albert Ernest Flemming

With an Introduction by
Dr. Victor Lange

ROUTLEDGE
NEW YORK

Reprinted in 1990 by
Routledge, an imprint of
Routledge, Chapman and Hall, Inc.
29 West 35th St.
New York, N.Y. 10001

Second expanded edition published in the United States of
America in 1985 by Methuen, Inc., 29 West 35th Street,
New York, N.Y. 10001
First edition published by Golden Smith Associates, Florida.

A series of these translations appeared in the Home Forum
section of the *Christian Science Monitor,*
Boston, Mass., between 1980 through 1984.

Reproductions by courtesy of the Ernst Barlach Museum,
Güstrow, German Democratic Republic.

Cover illustration:
Family of Saltimbanques; Pablo Picasso;
National Gallery of Art,
Washington D.C.; Chester Dale Collection

Library of Congress Cataloging-in-Publication Data

Rilke, Rainer Maria, 1875–1926.
  Rainer Maria Rilke.

  1. Rilke, Rainer Maria, 1875–1926—Translations,
English.   I. Flemming, Albert Ernest.   II. Title.
PT2635.I65A2352   1985   831'.912   85-18890
ISBN 0-416-01211-6   ISBN 0-415-90405-6 (pbk.)

Printed in the United States of America

ACKNOWLEDGMENTS

In addition to the appreciation of my family in England, I would like to express my thanks for the encouragement given to me by many friends. Without such encouragement I would not have had the incentive to continue these translations.

Among these friends I wish to mention the following:

Dr. and Mrs. Robin Anderson
Dr. and Mrs. Wesley B. Argo
Mrs. Henri Bercovici
Dr. Margaret Bowlby
Mme. Norah Drewett de Kresz
Mrs. Rosalyn Goldberg
Rev. Father Arthur C. Kreinheder, CSC,
Mrs. Patricia Love
Dr. Albert F. Maier
Mr. and Mrs. John Mallett
Dr. Robert A. Moorehead
Mr. Earle Moss
Dr. Arnold Orlick
Mr. Ross Parmenter
Mr. Steven Ratiner
Mrs. Walter E. Rogan
Mrs. Adeline Rosenblatt
Mr. Graeme Smith
Mrs. Elizabeth Tait
Professor Dr. Friedrich Weinhardt

IN MEMORY

The translation of
"Almond trees in bloom"
("Mandelbäume in Blüte")
was composed in memory
of Albert Flemming's brother
GEORGE,
who died in his adopted Spain,
Málaga, August 27, 1982.

To
LaDonis James King
in gratitude
for the happy journey

AUTHOR'S PREFACE

The idea of translating the poetry of Rainer Maria Rilke into English goes back to the thirteen years spent in Southern Germany at private schools, college and the state conservatory of music. His poetry, prose works and revealing letters had a decisive influence on my formative years. It was then that I began my first translations for the enjoyment of my family and friends back home in London.

Years later, when serving in the Royal Canadian Army's Auxiliary Services during World War II, I was asked by fellow officers and men to introduce them to Rilke's poetry: friends who were stationed in far-off places, in submarines, the Atlantic Ferry Command, on mine sweepers in the Caribbean; American friends on lonely Pacific atolls, in isolated military hospitals in the Californian desert, taking care of the endless arrival of war casualties. Rilke's poetry provided a spiritual comfort that they desperately needed during those trying years. Some of these friends lost their lives. . . .

After retiring to Florida, I was asked by a friend to translate Rilke's poem "Roman Fountain at the Villa Borghese". He was so impressed with the translation that he suggested I submit it to the *Christian Science Monitor*'s Home Forum. The poem was accepted and published in 1980 and was subsequently followed by other poems during the following four years.

With this encouragement and the enthusiastic acceptance of the poems by friends, I decided to present the translations in book form.

Some people may question the need for one more translation of Rilke's poetry. My justification is based on the inadequacy of many translations. Rilke's meaning is often obscured, sometimes totally misrepresented. Some translators seem to work solely with a dictionary at their side and do not have sufficient knowledge of the German language where a word may have various meanings just as we find in the English language. Others try desperately to make the lines rhyme, an impossible task, and thereby choose wrong or unsuitable words. The sad truth is that a poem in any language cannot be rendered verbatim in rhythm and rhyme into another language.

The translator faces a demanding task as a recreating artist and writer. He is expected to represent faithfully the original text, but he must succeed in doing this in his own language without being awkward. He must be alert in choosing vocabulary, syntax and cadence. If I may give an illustration using the word "Sunset". In "The Apple Orchard" the first strophe ends on the word 'Sonnenuntergang' which is the German equivalent of 'Sunset'. To achieve the same five syllables with an equal distribution of the evenly divided accent I chose "... watch the sun go down". Then, too, Rilke invents words that cannot be found in any German dictionary and you work hard to search for his intended meaning. And sometimes you discover that a word has its origin in a no longer used medieval expression.

Often his language is so compact that at times it seems like having to unravel patiently a skein of wool to find the beginning thread of understanding.

Rilke was foremost a lyric poet. Translations of his poems must *flow,* even though the lines' rhythm may have to change and the endings do not rhyme. The *'song',* the *'meaning'* must be as close to the original as possible—and that is the difficult task that faces the translator. This is why a sound knowledge of German is essential.

Redington Shores, Florida
Spring 1983.

Be patient toward all that
is unsolved in your heart
and try to love the questions
themselves.

Rainer Maria Rilke
(from his letters)

INTRODUCTION

BY DR VICTOR LANGE

In that extraordinary group of Austro-German writers who emerged at the turn of the century to create within some 30 years a literary canon of the highest imaginative and philosophical rank, Rainer Maria Rilke is one of the most remarkable. Born in Prague in 1875, unhappy in a childhood determined by an eccentric mother, he spent some years (1886–1891) at two Austrian military academies and completed his education in Linz and Prague. It was in the years between 1891 and 1897 that René (as he was called until 1897) wrote, and soon published, his first collection of poetry (*Leben und Lieder / Life and Songs,* 1894; *Larenopfer / Offerings of Diverse Poems,* 1895; *Traumgekrönt / Crowned by Dreams,* 1896), undistinguished sentimental poems, imitative of Heine and minor contemporary poets, vague in perception and unsure in theme and imagery. There was certainly little indication of the intensity of feeling and reflection or the sharpness of observation that were to become the conspicuous quality of his later work. In his single-minded determination to clarify and develop his talent (and to stylize his private life) in pointed opposition to the bourgeois conventions of the time, he followed the admired models of the French symbolist poets, of Wilde, Swinburne and d'Annuncio, of Maeterlink, Stefan George and the young Hofmannsthal. A certain detachment, an aversion to maintaining ties of permanent friendship, a restless compulsion to travel, his preference for works of art rather than direct human encounters as the source of his imaginative work, all these remained to the end characteristic of Rilke's life.

In 1896 he moved to Munich and there, stimulated by the painters and writers who lived in that lively center of art and literature, he read widely, especially the works of Jens Peter Jacobsen, and met, among others, the novelist Jacob Wassermann who introduced him to Lou Andreas-Salomé. This remarkable woman, fourteen years his senior, born in St. Petersburg, was a friend of Nietzsche, of Gerhart Hauptmann, Wedekind, Schnitzler and later (1911) a close collaborator of Freud's. She was the author of two religious tracts in which she describes the loss of belief in a personal God and her faith, instead, in an all-embracing, all-sustaining Eros.

It was Lou Andreas-Salomé's influence that profoundly affected Rilke's view of himself, of his scope as a poet and of the relationship between his sensibility and the world of concrete reality. What had so far been a mere impressionistic accumulation of miscellaneous and momentary experiences now became in each poetic statement an intensely circumscribed field of introspection or of vision and contemplation, focussed in remembered figures, incidents and objects. The character and the fervor of his love for Lou Salomé is rendered (1897) in the ecstatic poem that opens the present volume: "Extinguish Thou my eyes . . ."

In the company of Lou and her husband, he spent some time in Berlin, and (1898) in Florence, receptive at all times to aesthetic impressions, drawing from them a religious commitment to producing images of a kind of piety that "creates" God instead of only regarding Him as an absolute postulate. In 1899 he published (and in

1909 revised) his first substantial collection of poetry (*Mir Zur Feier / For Me to Celebrate,* later *Die Frühen Gedichte / Early Poems*), less vaguely preoccupied with musical or picturesque effects, more precise in outline and, tentatively, anticipating certain motifs—"God," "Word" or "Angel"—that were to recur and grow more subtle in his later work.

Rilke's intellectual and poetic horizon was immeasurably enlarged by two journeys to Russia with Professor and Mrs. Andreas, during which he joined in the Orthodox Easter celebrations in the Kremlin and met Tolstoy as well as the painters Pasternak and Repin. Deeply affected by the profound religious faith of the Russian people, he wrote a number of shorter works that for long assured his popularity: *The Tale of the Love and Death of Cornet Christopher Rilke; The Book of Monastic Life; Stories of the Good Lord* and the poems that were later collected in *Das Stundenbuch* (*The Book of Prayers*). Especially a second visit to Russia (1900) deepened his affection for the simple life of peasants and monks whose devotion he admired and sought to emulate as a form of daily involvement in the divine creation.

"Russia," Rilke was to say at the end of his life, "was in a certain sense the foundation of my ways of experiencing and of absorbing the world": it was not so much, he meant, an aesthetic as an existential progression. Indeed, the fascination with the romantic mysticism that he witnessed in Russia encouraged in him a tendency towards indistinct and simple-minded religious sentiments and, in turn, a kind of poetry more pure in heart than scrupulous. For two years, having parted from Lou Andreas-Salomé, he settled in the artists colony of Worpswede, entered into a brief and uncongenial marriage, wrote occasional poems and reviews, but terminated this unproductive interlude in 1902 and moved to Paris in order to write a biography of the sculptor Rodin.

Here he lived until 1914, twelve years of extraordinary consequence for his development as a poet. "Paris," he concluded the sentence in which he speaks first of Russia, "Paris—the incomparable—was the basis of my will to deal with shapes and figures." He had for some time been determined to rid his poetry of all merely narrative or private elements, and in the collection of poems written in Worpswede, *The Book of Images* (*Das Buch der Bilder*) he aims (as yet without complete success) at a concentrated perception, at giving significance to an event by gathering in the poem the sum of patient reflection and metaphorical speech. As we withdraw, he seems to argue, from the familiar world that we take for granted, we learn to "see" implications and structures that bring about a rich and distinctive universe, a "world" of significant relationships.

The first years in Paris, with occasional journeys to Rome, Denmark and Sweden, decisively altered the manner and quality of his poetic work. The poems which he now included in the enlarged version of the *Book of Prayers* (1905) are appealing in their measured musical language and their lively pictorial material. Despite the title, the theme that binds these poems together is secular and not monastic. It is the life and procedure of the artist, constantly tested, it is the praise of art, of writing and of painting, and the acts of singing, confessing and enunciating—all means of giving concreteness to the reality of the divine—that form the tenor of this collection.

Rilke's close association with Rodin and his admiration for Cézanne produced that astonishing disavowal of mere incidental inspiration and indistinct poetic effusiveness and brought about, instead, the firm and "objective" manner that soon produced poetry of the most severe perfection. Rodin taught him the craft of drawing the utmost meaning from the precise rendering of a simple object, the evocation of essential features by an exact conveying of the nuances and the translucency of the surface. What he learned from Cézanne was the importance of order and design, a careful procedure of structuring each image, each gesture, each line or stanza. The simple object rather than any random association of impressions now seemed the most expressive and concise vehicle for his poetic intentions. In *New Poems* (*Neue Gedichte*) two chronologically arranged cycles deal with representative moments in the history of European culture, the Bible, classical antiquity, the Middle Ages and the Renaissance; but many pieces are specifically devoted to single objects. If "Roman Fountain," "The Merry-Go-Round," the superb "Archaic Torso of Apollo" are in a strict sense "Dinggedichte" ("thing-poems"), others deal with animals, with mythological figures or, like "Self-portrait, 1906" with subjects that seem to aim at achieving in words something like the equivalent of a piece of sculpture. The celebrated prototype of such concentrated statements, severely reduced to an apostrophe of their essence, is "The Panther," the first of the "Dinggedichte," written in 1902. Here and elsewhere time seems no longer in flux, it is not an intimation of human temporality or the blurring thrust of development, but the element in which present abundance is fathomed, undisturbed or momentarily arrested in the act of memory.

Time and the recognition of its finality in death, death forever present in life, is one of the central themes of Rilke's most complex, yet engrossing piece of prose fiction. *The Notebooks of Malte Laurids Brigge* is the account of a sensitive young Danish nobleman who experiences in Paris the extremes of the human condition, the most intense physical disgust, total loneliness, the beginnings of madness and an elusive but devastating sense of anguish. Darkness and negativity, the vile and the absurd, determine the haunting images and scenes of this document of self-doubt and spiritual agony. The years of its composition—1904 to 1910— were for Rilke a time of continuous travel and unsettled life. Baudelaire and Cézanne now provide the elements of an aesthetic creed which no longer aims at the achievement of beauty in the traditional sense, but at lucidity and a fearless rendering of states of mind that recognizes in the negative and terrifying the evidence of a totality of Being. Neither the world nor the self can here be conveyed as an organic whole or, indeed, as altogether coherent. Rilke's narrative devices are, in consequence, the instruments of disjointedness and discontinuity; the flow of events is circuitous, the central character who, like the hero of Dostoevsky's *Notes from the Underground,* cannot comprehend himself as an intelligible human entity, is the sum of the incidents of horror and shock that he must force himself to confront.

Various forms of death and disease, strange memories, dreams and apparitions elaborate the features of a world whose surface is fractured and whose fragments offer documents of life intelligible only if we succeed in denying temporality, if we exist not within the confines of chronology but in an awareness of what Rilke calls the "inherent rhythm" of objects or events. The work concludes with a curious reinterpretation of the parable of the Prodigal Son, the legend, as it is here understood, of "one who did not want to be loved," who leaves his self-centered family in order not to have to share their "mendacious" life. Abroad he learns to live without possessions or ambition and devotes himself to the love of God, pure, and unencumbered by a false faith in response or reward. He returns home to "re-live" his youth, indifferent to the family's intrusive offerings of affection, and unwilling to let the love of others constrain and limit him as an object; he is ready only for the love of God, but, so end the *Notebooks, "He* was not yet willing." *Malte Laurids Brigge* is one of the most disquieting and searching works of modern fictional prose; Rilke insisted that it represented "less a descent into negativity than a strange and dark ascent to a neglected and remote part of Heaven. . . ."

For two years after completing the *Notebooks* Rilke again travelled extensively, uncertain of his ultimate effectiveness as a poet. Some of these journeys, such as three months in Egypt, were to supply metaphorical motifs for his later poetry. Through the generosity of the Princess of Thurn und Taxis he was able to stay from October 1911 to May 1912 at Castle Duino near Trieste and there composed *The Life of the Virgin Mary* (*Das Marienleben*), a cycle of fifteen poems in which, drawing on pictures by the Spanish artist Ribadaniera, he celebrates the sensitive and intuitive strength of Mary, Joseph's more commonplace obtuseness and the Savior's exalted career: "You stood apart and overshadowed me . . ." ("Pietà"). Once again it is the "great angel" whose appearance mediates between human sensibility and the realm of transcendent faith. That image of the Angel recurs throughout Rilke's work, but its invocation in these poems coincides on the very day, 21 January 1912, with the writing in an astonishing burst of inspiration, of the first of the *Duino Elegies,* Rilke's greatest achievement, with its desperate opening question: "Who, if I cried out, would hear me among the angels' hierarchies?"

The First and Second Elegy, the beginning of the Third and parts of the Sixth, the Ninth and the Tenth were written within a few weeks at Duino; he paused for a year, constantly preoccupied with the slowly emerging cycle, traveled in 1913 in Spain, lived in 1914 in Paris, produced the Fourth Elegy in Munich in November of 1915 and completed the work in February of 1922 at the tiny "castle" Muzot near Sierre in Switzerland where he was to die four years later.

These ten spacious and intricate poems are "elegies" not in the formal sense of a series of stanzas in distichs; they articulate, rather, the thematic movement, largely in free verse, from inadequacy and doubt in the testimonial power of the human performance to the acceptance of a world of infinitely "telling" concreteness and an ultimate rendering of it in acts of praise and rejoicing. The beginning of the Tenth Elegy offers the summary of the cycle as a whole and attempts at the same time an appropriate response to the initial cry of the first: "That some day, emerging at last from the terrifying vision, I may burst into jubilant praise to assenting angels!"

The myth, or symbolism, of the "Angels" elaborates at once the austere projection of an absolute existence beyond human inquietudes and inadequacies, and envisages exemplary models of hope in accomplishing and affirming a sustaining sense of life. The topics of the *Elegies* range from the potter on the Nile to Rilke's own present, from the exploration of consciousness to speculations about the imaginatively "knowing" plants and animals, articulating their special awareness of being. These themes, concentrated in an astounding variety of images, amplify and paraphrase the subject matter of the cycle: the limitations of human existence, imprisoned in temporality and the inescapable circumstances of being, and instances of transcending it in acts of total dedication. While the *Elegies* lack the unity of a single intellectual argument and share with other great poems of our time a deliberate hermetic convolution, irregular syntax and surprising turns of language, inversion and alliteration, they are linked by profuse verbal or metaphorical variations and associations; they are, above all, an account of the poetic process and ultimately amount to a document intended to justify the achievements of art and poetry as means of giving coherence to a world no longer stabilized by traditional systems of belief. "Saying" and "performing" are therefore the two recurring tropes or figures of thought that establish or resolve the juncture of life and death, of lover and beloved, of inner and outer reality, of spectator and artist. These are the very tensions from which the poetic act is born. To love as the ultimate offering by which human actions and feelings can be transcended, the *Elegies* return again and again. It is the specific topic of the first three and the central motif of the first.

Here, in our "interpreted" world, the human being is without certainty and threatened by the restraints of temporality and the impermanence of love; yet, praise of the highest intensity of feeling, and an acceptance of the passing character of life may enhance our existence. Great examples of love, even though unfulfilled (such as that of the poetess Gaspara Stampa) will increase our understanding: "should not their oldest sufferings finally become more fruitful for us?" (First Elegy). As well as the memory of love, it is the continuing presence of those who died young, those recorded on the tablet in Santa Maria Formosa, who should give us courage: they have "accomplished" their death, for "being dead is hard work and full of retrieving before one can gradually feel a trace of eternity." The mythical dirge at the death of Linos filled the space emptied by his passing with those "vibrations which now enrapture and comfort and help us."

The serene and perfect Existence of the Angel is, in the Second Elegy (thematically related to the First), contrasted with the volatile life of man who, unlike those Beings, must bear the burden of an infinite tension between subject and object, the self and the world: "we, when we feel, evaporate." Lovers, "each satisfied in the other," are again invoked as instances of a potential state of peace and of immunity to the constraints of time. Love which seeks immediate satisfaction—this is the argument of the Third Elegy—is insufficient: it is— in terms and concepts which Rilke borrowed from Freud—the unconscious and subconscious erotic drive, that "hidden guilty river-god of the blood," of which we cannot "speak" to the Angel. Here, as in the Fourth Elegy, it is the conflict so frequently treated in Rilke's later work, between reflection and an immediate awareness of the true "contour of feeling," that drives the poet to a profound sort of self-scrutiny. "Before his own heart's curtain" he seeks to differentiate the impulses of his awareness. When the imaginary stage empties, when his heart is drained of feeling, when death enters with a grey draft of emptiness, he continues to watch: but to the hollow performance of the actor he now prefers puppets in their specific and not "masked" character, and with utmost concentration calls forth an "Angel," that being of infinite consciousness and, joined in this visionary space, the puppet who is wholly devoid of consciousness. In this speculative union, "What we separate can come together by our very presence." With a Rousseauean flourish Rilke exempts only children and the dying from the fateful schism of mind and emotion: the child who, when it must die, contains death, "the whole of death, even before life has begun." But this, the elegy concludes, is for us, the divided and oscillating creatures, an "indescribable condition."

If the Fourth Elegy, written in November of 1915, is the most bitter, the Fifth is the richest in imagery and the most coherent in its argument. It was (in February of 1922) the last to be written and forms the pivotal piece of the series. For its central motif, Rilke recalled a performance of Père Rollin's troupe of acrobats in Paris in 1907 and, in 1915, Picasso's "Les Saltimbanques" which he saw in Munich in the apartment of its owner, Hertha Koenig, to whom the elegy is dedicated. (This painting is now in the National Gallery in Washington.) Written at great speed, the poem is nevertheless an extraordinarily deliberate and unified composition. Two "voices," the voice of lament and that of praise, are here joined as though in counterpoint, and the Angel is, for once, called upon to consecrate and illuminate a human act. The acrobats as symbols of the human condition repeat with untiring virtuosity their mechanical number, their "endless leaping and tumbling," producing only "the thinnest veneer of a sham-smiling surface." In this sterile exercise the poet recognizes moments of tentative but authentic feeling: "suddenly in this wearisome No-where . . . suddenly the unspeakable place, where pure inadequacy incomprehensibly changes—leaps over into that empty 'too-much.' " The vacuous and restless motion is in fact propelled by death, disguised as Madame Lamort, the milliner who ceaselessly produces tawdry and glittering creations. The envisaged scene of a genuine life is the "place of which we did not know" where, before the assembly of the "countless silent dead" and "upon an indescribable carpet" love as the fulfillment of human self-realization, the "daring lofty leaps of heart-flight" may be performed and shown.

To the group of "pure" figures, to children, lovers and the early dead, the Sixth Elegy now adds the hero, whose life seems determined by an inner law, and is given actuality not in the "mere mobility" of the acrobats, but through one huge effort and without distraction even by love. The hero recognizes no dichotomy between life and death, indeed from a certain perspective, "fulfills" his heroic character only after death. The five exquisite stanzas end with a summary of motifs that have occurred throughout the previous poems: "whenever the Hero stormed through the stays of love, each heartbeat intended for him could only lift him beyond it; turning away, he stood at the end of the smiles—transfigured."

The mood of despair and doubt that configures the course and material of the first six elegies changes in the remaining four to a mood of almost exuberant affirmation of the here and now, a paean to nature and the human existence—even at the present "torpid turn of the world" in which, "ever diminishing, vanishes what is outside . . ." we must resolve to keep "still recognizable form" and thus learn that "nowhere can world exist but within. Life passes in transformation." This is one of the metaphors that become the key to Rilke's philosophy of "internalizing" the ingredients of the experienced world: "Weltinnenraum" is the term that points, not to any abstract or mystical diminishing of reality but, on the contrary, to its reconstruction and absorption within an "inner space," to an intense concentration on the precisely envisaged and explored object, "an invisible rearising in us." This act of transformation is further explored in the following elegies, especially the Ninth, in which, recognizing the lamentable transitoriness of our life and the contradictions in human nature, the appropriate task of "transforming" experience must be made communicable through "saying," the act, at its most intense, of poetic creation. "Here," Rilke insists, "is the time for the tellable, here is its home. Speak and proclaim." In memorable lines he justifies his resolution to testify to the world:

For the Wanderer does not bring home from the mountain slope a handful of earth to the valley, untellable earth, but an experienced word, a pure word, the yellow and blue gentian. Are we perhaps *here* just for saying: House, Bridge, Well, Gate, Jug, Olive Tree, Window,—possibly Pillar, Tower? . . . but for saying, remember . . .

It is in the Tenth, the final elegy, that lament and rejoicing are brought into balance: "That some day," it begins, "emerging at last from the terrifying vision, I may burst into jubilant praise to assenting angels!" The insight which suffering, "our winter's foliage, somber evergreen" has produced, has joined sorrow and truth, those premises of our life and death. The grim and satirical verses in which once more the inauthentic and pointless commotion of a mythical "Leid-Stadt," the city of pain, points to the mindless indifference towards suffering and death, beyond which "reality," the realm of significant life, begins, the transition to death and to the "landscape of lamentation." Here, in a setting reminiscent of Egypt, the "Leidland," the land of pain, in which, in the mountains of primal pain, the "Fountain-head of Joy" receives the young man who has died in early youth and who now passes into a land of fulfill-ment beyond sound and speech. The elegy ends with an octave of simple and natural images that suggest a bal-ancing of rising and falling, of happiness and sorrow, of life and death.

The *Duino Elegies* in their taut concatenation of images, the wide range of their, at times opaque, symbol-ism, and the singularly challenging filiations of their lan-guage, is one of the most demanding works of modern European literature; they have added a dimension of prophetic and mythical poetry to German literature that echoes the voices of Klopstock and Hölderlin and antici-pates the crystallized verse of Celan.

Rilke was conscious of the enormous effort he made in February 1922 to complete (with the Fifth) the cycle of the *Elegies* and to offer in these poems the sum total of his poetic vision. What followed, during the four years before his death of leukemia, was a prodigious series of occasional poems that seem to testify to a sense of ending, an awareness of life in the shadow of death, a compulsion to speak in images as rich in spiritual resonance as any in his previous work. Although often casual in subject matter they nevertheless paraphrase in memorable poetic gestures Rilke's ceaseless resolve to move towards meaning in a world of lost certainty, where only the particular and concrete moment of recognition, of sight and listening hold out the promise of fulfillment. "Meaning," this must be recognized, was for Rilke not the achieved acceptance of an absolute, or the epitome of a systematic creed—he was in fact pointedly skeptical of any orthodox Christian postulates—but the result of contemplating and comprehending the structure, the totality of an object or a situation, an act of insight made possible essentially in and through the performance of language.

While Rilke completed the *Elegies* he produced, within a few days, "as though they were dictated," a series of *Sonnets to Orpheus,* more than 50 poems arranged in two corresponding parts. He here evokes the myth of Orpheus, the inventor of hymnic songs of praise, but specifies the general thrust of the traditional association by exploring the instrumental senses of saying and listening and altogether returning throughout these sonnets to what might be called the existential polarities of life and death, faith and doubt, sleep and waking, unity and discrepancy. In the *Sonnets* these disparate states are no longer seen as challenges beyond comprehension or resolution; they are now accepted as inherent in the human condition, as relationships to be courageously experienced and as the appropriate topics of testimonial speech and praise. Just as Orpheus, in the midst of death, enchanted the netherworld with his song, Rilke's sonnets are exercises in acceptance and celebration. Their tone is exuberant rather than plaintive, the pace of their language lively, their phrasing often hectic; the listener to be addressed is no longer the Angel but the responsive reader. The organs of perception, eye, ear and mouth, supply the recurring images; sleep and waking, breath and heartbeat circumscribe the elements that offer insight and reassurance. The voice of the first Sonnet draws us urgently into the topography which promises "a new beginning"; the joined realms of space and sound, of object and movement, of the interdependent modes of singing and silence, the magic presence of Orpheus:

> There rose a tree. O magic transcendence!
> Orpheus sings! And in the ear a tree!
> Silence reigned. Yet even in this silence
> a new beginning dawned and changes came.
>
> For creatures stepped soundlessly from clearings
> of forests and left lair and nest behind;
> and all this happened not through fear or fright
> that made them so intent on keeping still:
>
> the better to listen. Howling, crying,
> roaring seemed small within their hearts. And where
> there was scarcely a hut to shelter them. . . .
>
> a hiding place out of their darkest longings,
> with an entrance gate whose structure trembled, . . .
> there you created temples in their ears!

"The temple in the ear," the place of communication and worship, is the gift of the singer, of Orpheus, who, as the ninth Sonnet puts it, is the supreme witness of life and death:

Only who holds the lyre
among the shadows
may be allowed to render
the infinite praise.

Only who with the dead shared
their own poppy seeds
will never lose the sound of
their softest of tones.

The reflection at times may
seem blurred in the pool:
know the image.

Only in the two-fold realm
do voices become
eternal and mild.

Orpheus is the "fountain-head, whose never silent mouth / speaks endlessly of all that's great and pure . . ." (fifteenth Sonnet).

The doubt in any available mode that might transcend the impermanence of life, so emphatically the theme of the *Elegies,* is in the fifth Sonnet dispelled and memorably replaced by the praise of Orpheus who is part of a finite and transitory world. He is the rose in one of his metamorphoses; while he must leave, his word surpasses his being here. "Does Orpheus belong here?"

is the question which the Sixth Sonnet categorically denies: he is the singer of life as well as death, that is to say, he asserts the unity of life. And as he exists in two realms, he becomes the ultimate witness of that "Doppelbereich," of that interplay of life and death, for which Rilke throughout his work sought adequate images, and which is here illuminated in sharper focus and conveyed as a more positive vision than in any of his earlier poetry. Praise, he had often said, is not merely the corollary of lament, but the act without which all lament is vain and self-indulgent. In a previous poem, "O tell us, poet, what it is you do?" (see *Collected Poems*) the question is posed in radical terms: "In the midst of deadly turmoil, what helps you endure, and how do you survive?"—"Das Tödliche und Ungetüme, / Wie hältst du's aus, wie nimmst du's hin?" Rilke's confident answer is: "I praise,"—"Ich rühme."

Certain that he had fulfilled his most formidable task as a poet, and aware, during the few remaining years of his life, of his fatal disease, Rilke continued to write, often in a haunting state of inspiration and now with an impressive mastery of linguistic and formal resources, an extraordinary number of superb poems, many of them in French. These were not the first in that language but now as before indicative of a strong sense of affinity to Baudelaire and Mallarmé, and of his friendship with Gide, Claudel and, above all, Valéry, whose "Cimetière Marin" he had translated in 1921. In all these the familiar themes and metaphors recur, simplified and, indeed, elegantly turned into lucid vehicles of serenity and assent. His last poem, the final entry in his notebook, written two weeks before his death on 29 December 1926, is the anguished sequence of stanzas: "Come thou, thou last one, whom I recognize."

.   .   .

Neither the person nor the poet Rilke is easily as-
sessed or defined. From the first unhappy years and the
awkward and sentimental early efforts at writing poetry,
his life was wholly dedicated to the pursuit of art, the determination to render in his work an impulse at once
aesthetic and religious, that would draw meaning from
the world about him and give testimony to the inextric-
ably interwoven experiences of affirmation and despair,
inadequacy and achievement, belief in the present moment and the compulsion to transcend it.

In its totality, Rilke's work reflects his personal life
and disposition, as well as, and perhaps even more so,
the curiously pessimistic historical climate that became
palpable at the turn of the century. He felt and recorded
the pervasive doubt in the strength or adequacy of a
modern rationalistic society, and shared the double per-
spectives which since Schopenhauer and Nietzsche had
become widely accepted axioms of life—the withdrawal
into a melancholy lyricism and, concomitant with it, an
assertion of life in its most abundant form, defiant of the
debilitating restrictions of bourgeois conventions.

He was extraordinarily sensitive to the deeply dis-
turbing signs of this cultural unrest and, without any
sustained interest in theoretical discourse, learned to
draw conclusions from the work of contemporary artists,
of painters such as Cézanne, sculptors such as Rodin and
writers such as Flaubert, Jacobsen and Tolstoy, but
above all from the French symbolist poets. The first decisive encounter with a form of life that seemed to him
"complete" and exemplary was his sharing of the reli-

31

gious ethos of Russian peasants; the subsequent years in Paris changed the direction of his spiritual and aesthetic aspirations. While not at all inclined to enter into intimate and responsible friendships, he was eager to reach out to women and men who seemed to him receptive and congenial. But it is not too much to say that after uncertain and juvenile beginnings, his life was devoted with single-minded conviction and determination to the articulation of his experiences in poetry of an ever more demanding sort. "Poetry," he was to say, "is more important than any human relationship." The musical charm of his verse remained one of the fascinating, at times dangerously seductive, elements of his poetry and, together with an often imprecise but vaguely moving allusiveness, one of the chief reasons for his extraordinary popularity.

Rilke was slow in maturing, slow in overcoming his early sentimentality and the ease of his mystical posture; slow also in repressing his obsessive fondness for poetic ornament and the glibness of his play with words, his forced assonances, alliterations and rhymes. Yet, what was to become the signature of Rilke's work was an incomparable virtuosity in inventing and linking metaphors and the ability to produce the most subtle and evocative shades of speech in poetry that is, unlike the work of most of his European contemporaries, almost entirely self-contained and self-referential. From the beginning his visual sensibility was remarkable: it was to be the powerful instrument and medium of his later accomplished poetry—*"Sehen"* and *"Schauen"* recur as the most productive impulses of his efforts at "perceiving," recovering and, in his terms, "creating" the phenomenal world. The lilt and melodiousness of his thin but fluid youthful verses turned, as his self-denying mastery increased, into that characteristic postulate of "praise," the echoing of the music of Orpheus, the singing of assent to the created universe.

Rilke's much-quoted line in the Seventh Elegy, "Hiersein ist herrlich" ("to be here, alive, is wonderful"), is, indeed, the key to his increasingly unambiguous faith in the totality of a profoundly perceptive life, a life in which negativity and hope, the awareness of temporality and altogether the full understanding of the frailty of existence are recognized not as agonizing alternatives but as relationships within one inexhaustible whole. The changing function of the concept of death, that dominant and constant image of his entire work, is symptomatic of the slow shift in his perspective and assessment of life: life with the terror of its finality is increasingly given meaning and intelligibility as death is accepted as one of its most powerful dimensions. Grief for the dead was for that reason one of Rilke's most moving experiences: a number of "Requiem" poems testify to the challenge which mourning imposes upon the living.

It is in the Ninth Elegy that the interdependence of life and death, but even more of joy and suffering, resolved in the act of praise, is most memorably stated:

Zwischen den Hämmern besteht unser Herz,/
wie die Zunge zwischen den Zähnen,/
die doch, dennoch, die preisende bleibt.

Our heart exists between hammers, / like the
tongue between our teeth, in spite of which/
the tongue remains always the bestower of praise.

In the *Elegies* and the *Sonnets* Rilke had moved far from the neo-romantic word-painting of his first collections, beyond even the more sharply defined vision of a world of describable objects and figures in *Neue Gedichte* to *"Anschauen"* and *"Preisen"* ("perceiving" and "praising"), to the assurance of hymnic exaltation and the triumphant accomplishment of expressive speech, giving shape to the elemental impulses of our modern life, anguish, hope and acceptance. He fulfilled what in *Malte Laurids Brigge* he had defined as the essential prerequisite of a poet's accomplishment:

"Alas, those verses one writes in youth aren't much. One should wait and gather meaning and sweetness all his life, a long one if possible, and then maybe at the end he might write ten good lines. For poetry isn't, as people imagine, merely feelings (these come soon enough); it is experiences. To write one line, a man ought to see many cities, people, and things; he must learn to know animals and the way of birds in the air, and should be aware of the gesture with which little flowers open in the morning. One must be able to think back the way to unknown places, to unexpected encounters and to partings long foreseen, to days of childhood ... and to parents whom one had to hurt when they brought us joy (it was joy for another), to days on the sea, yes to the sea, to nights of travel that flew with the stars, and one must have memories of many nights of love, no two alike ... and the screams of women in childbed ... one must have sat by the dying, one must have sat by the dead in a room with open windows and intermittent noises. ... But it is not enough to have memories. One must be able to forget them and have much patience until they come again, and memories as such are not enough: only when they become blood within us, and glances and gestures, nameless and no longer differentiated from us, only then it can happen that in a rare hour the first word of a verse may arise and come forth. . . ."

Victor Lange,
Princeton University,
1985.

CONTENTS

COLLECTED POEMS COVERING THE YEARS FROM
1906 to 1926:
*(GESAMMELTE GEDICHTE AUS DEN JAHREN
1906 bis 1926:)*

46

LIST OF ILLUSTRATIONS AND CREDITS

FROM THE BOOK OF PRAYERS

(DAS STUNDENBUCH)

BERLIN - 1899

EXTINGUISH THOU MY EYES

*E*xtinguish Thou my eyes: I still can see Thee,
deprive my ears of sound: I still can hear Thee,
and without feet I still can come to Thee,
and without voice I still can call to Thee.

Sever my arms from me, I still will hold Thee
with all my heart as with a single hand,
arrest my heart, my brain will keep on beating,
and should Thy fire at last my brain consume,
the flowing of my blood will carry Thee.

THE SEEKER

I live my life in ever widening circles,
each superseding all the previous ones.
Perhaps I never shall succeed in reaching
the final circle, but attempt I will.

I circle around God, the ancient tower,
and have been circling for a thousand years,
and still I do not know: am I a falcon,
a storm, or a continuing great song?

DEDICATION

I have great faith in all things not yet spoken.
I want my deepest pious feelings freed.
What no one yet has dared to risk and warrant
will be for me a challenge I must meet.

If this presumptuous seems, God, may I be forgiven.
For what I want to say to you is this:
my efforts shall be like a driving force,
quite without anger, without timidness
as little children show their love for you.

With these outflowings, river-like, with deltas
that spread like arms to reach the open sea,
with the recurrent tides that never cease
will I acknowledge you, will I proclaim you
as no one ever has before.

And if this should be arrogance, so let me
arrogant be to justify my prayer
that stands so serious and so alone
before your forehead, circled by the clouds.

O LORD, GRANT EVERYONE HIS SOVEREIGN DEATH

O Lord, grant everyone his sovereign death,
a dying that extinguishes a life
which gave him love, significance and dearth.

For we are but the sheltering husk and leaf.
The great Death which each harbors in himself,
that is the Fruit round which all else resolves.

FROM THE BOOK OF IMAGES

(DAS BUCH DER BILDER)

(1902 and 1906)

AT SUNDOWN

*S*lowly the evening starts to change her raiments
for veils held up by rows of distant trees.
You watch how gradually the landscape's contours change,
some rising heavenward as others downward fall;

leaving you alone, to neither quite belonging,
nor quite as dark as houses silent keep,
nor quite so sure beseeching the eternal
as that which nightly turns to star and rises ---

and leaving you (impossible to disentangle)
your life, fearful, gigantic and still ripening,
which, now limited, now comprehending,
alternatingly becomes stone in you and star.

LAMENT

O how all things are far removed
and long have passed away.
I do believe the star,
whose light my face reflects,
is dead and has been so
for many thousand years.

I had a vision of a passing boat
and heard some voices say disquieting things.
I heard a clock strike in some distant house . . . .
but in which house? . . . .

I long to quiet my anxious heart
and stand beneath the sky's immensity.
I long to pray . . . .
And one of all the stars
must still exist.
I do believe that I would know
which one alone
endured,
and which like a white city stands
at the ray's end shining in the heavens.

A CHILDHOOD MEMORY

*A*dvancing darkness lent a richness to the room
in which the boy sat hiding, waiting silently.
And as the mother entered, dreamlike, suddenly
a glass kept trembling in the silent cabinet.
She sensed the room's betrayal of her presence
and saw her son and kissed him: Are you here?. . .
Then both looked shyly toward the piano,
where many an evening she had played a song
that strangely moved and touched him deep inside.

He sat quite still. His wide gaze never leaving
the hands that seemed quite bent down by her rings.
As if they were through heavy snowdrifts ploughing
while traversing the whiteness of the keys.

AUTUMN DAY

*L*ord, it is time. The summer's greatness ended.
Cast down upon the sundials cooling shades
and let the winds blow wild across the fields.

Command those tardy grapes to speed their ripening -
bless them with two more days of warming sun -
urge them to reach perfection, gain in sweetness -
that final heavy richness - on the vine.

Who's homeless now will never build a house.
Who's all alone will now so long remain,
will wake, will read and write long, lonely letters
and wander aimlessly through empty streets
and find no solace in the windblown leaves.

AUTUMN

The leaves are falling, falling from afar
as though from distant gardens in the heavens.
They fall reluctantly and loathe to leave.

So, too, the Earth is falling through the night
far from all stars down into solitude.

We all are falling. See this hand? It falls
as all things do respond to heaven's laws.

Yet there is One, our Lord, who holds this falling
in His so infinitely tender hands.

SOLEMN HOUR

*W*hoever now weeps somewhere in the world,
weeps without reason in the world,
weeps over me.

Whoever now laughs somewhere in the night,
laughs without reason in the night,
laughs at me.

Whoever now wanders somewhere in the world,
wanders without reason out in the world,
wanders towards me.

Whoever now dies somewhere in the world,
dies without reason in the world,
looks at me.

TO SAY BEFORE GOING TO SLEEP

I would like to sing someone to sleep,
have someone to sit by and be with.
I would like to cradle you and softly sing,
be your companion while you sleep or wake.
I would like to be the only person
in the house who knew: the night outside was cold.
And would like to listen here to you
and outside to the world and to the woods.

The clocks are striking, calling to each other,
and one can see right to the edge of time.
Outside the house a strange man is afoot
and a strange dog barks, wakened from his sleep.
Beyond that there is silence.

My eyes rest upon your face wide-open;
and they hold you gently, letting you go
when something in the dark begins to move.

THE ANGELS

They all have oh such tired mouths
and luminous souls without seams.
Sometimes a longing (as for sin)
goes wandering aimless through their dreams.

They all resemble one another
and in God's gardens silent keep
like many intervals and pauses
within his might and melody.

But when they open wide their wings,
they set the heaven's winds in motion
as if God with his sculpture-hands
were turning thoughtfully the giant pages
of Genesis' dark book of the beginning.

FOREBODING

I am like a flag unfurled facing far horizons.
I sense the oncoming winds through which I must survive,
while the things below me remain quiet, rest unmoving:
doors still close gently, and in the chimneys is silence,
windows do not tremble, and the dust lies undisturbed ---

Then I know the storm's approach and am as turbulent
as the sea. I flutter, strained to my limit; I reach
and fall back, only to hurl myself outward again
and find myself utterly alone in the great storm.

REMEMBRANCE

*A*nd you wait, keep waiting for that one thing
which would infinitely enrich your life:
the powerful, uniquely uncommon,
the awakening of dormant stones,
depths that would reveal you to yourself.

In the dusk you notice the book shelves
with their volumes in gold and in brown;
and you think of far lands you journeyed,
of pictures and of shimmering gowns
worn by women you conquered and lost.

And it comes to you all of a sudden:
That was it! And you arise, for you are
aware of a year in your distant past
with its fears and events and prayers.

THE NEIGHBOR

*S*trange violin, why do you follow me?
In how many foreign cities did you
speak of your lonely nights and those of mine.
Are you being played by hundreds? Or by one?

Do in all great cities men exist
who tormented and in deep despair
would have sought the river but for you?
And why does your playing always reach me?

Why is it that I am always neighbor.
to those lost ones who are forced to sing
and to say: Life is infinitely heavier
than the heaviness of all things.

NIGHT

*T*his night, agitated by the growing storm,
how it has suddenly expanded its dimensions ---,
that ordinarily would have gone unnoticed,
like a cloth folded, and hidden in the folds of time.

Where the stars give resistance it does not stop there,
neither does it begin within the forest's depths,
nor show upon the surface of my face
nor with your appearance.

The lamps keep swaying, fully unaware:
is our light *lying?*
Is night the only reality
that has endured through thousands of years?

THE POET

O hour of my muse: why do you leave me,
Wounding me by the wingbeats of your flight?
Alone: what shall I use my mouth to utter?

How shall I pass my days? And how my nights?

I have no one to love. I have no home.
There is no center to sustain my life.
All things to which I give myself grow rich
and leave me spent, impoverished, alone.

THE VISIONARY

I see from looking at the wind-tossed trees—
whose branches beat against my trembling windows—
the storm's effect that raged through sullen days,
and hear the far horizon speak of things
that I cannot endure without a friend,
nor love without a sister's presence.

There goes the storm, and in its wake he alters
shapes, drives on across the woods, across all time,
and everything looks as if it were ageless:
the landscape—like a verse out of the book of psalms—
remains unshaken, forceful and eternal.

How little are the things with which we wrestle.
What with us wrestles, how so much greater is!
If only we would let ourselves be conquered
as things are overcome by a great storm,
we would expand in space and need no names.

When we victorious are, it is over small things,
and though we won, it leaves us feeling small.
What is eternal, and what is not common,
does not *want* to be bent by human strength.
This is the angel who in ancient times
appeared to wrestlers of the Old Testament:
when his opponent's sinews during fighting
began to stretch like long metallic strands
that felt beneath the angel's gripping fingers
like singing strings responding with deep song.

Whoever was defeated by the angel -
and often one decided not to fight -
left walking proud and upright, full of strength,
and greater still for having felt the power
of these strong hands that molded him, as if
to change his shape.
For winning does not tempt him!
The secret of his growing lies in this:
by being totally defeated and disarmed
by even greater forces and their cause.

THE LAST SUPPER

They are assembled, astonished and disturbed,
round him, who like a sage resolved his fate,
and now leaves those to whom he most belonged,
leaving and passing by them like a stranger.
The loneliness of old comes over him
which helped mature him for his deepest acts;
now will he once again walk through the olive grove,
and those who love him still will flee before his sight.

To this last supper he has summoned them,
and (like a shot that scatters birds from trees)
their hands draw back from reaching for the loaves
upon his word: they fly across to him;
they flutter, frightened, round the supper table
searching for an escape. But he is present
everywhere like an all-pervading twilight-hour.

On seeing Leonardo da Vinci's
'Last Supper', Milan 1904.

THE VOICES

NINE PAGES WITH A TITLE PAGE

(DIE STIMMEN)

(NEUN BLÄTTER MIT EINEM TITELBLATT)

1906

TITLE PAGE

FOR "THE VOICES"

*T*he rich and the fortunate do well to keep silent,
for no one cares to know who and what they are.
But those in need must reveal themselves,
must say: I am blind,
or: I'm on the verge of going blind,
or: nothing goes well with me on earth,
or: I have a sickly child,
or: I have little to hold me together ...

And chances are this is not nearly enough.

And because people try to ignore them as they
pass by them: these unfortunate ones have to sing!

And at times one hears some excellent singing!

Of course, people differ in their tastes: some would
prefer to listen to choirs of boy-castrati.

But God Himself comes often and stays long,
when the castrati's singing disturbs Him.

THE SONG OF THE BEGGAR

I am always going from door to door,
whether in rain or heat,
and sometimes I will lay my right ear in
the palm of my right hand.
And as I speak my voice seems strange as if
it were alien to me,

for I'm not certain whose voice is crying:
mine or someone else's.
I cry for a pittance to sustain me.
The poets cry for more.

In the end I conceal my entire face
and cover both my eyes;
there it lies in my hands with all its weight
and looks as if at rest,
so no one may think I had no place where-
upon to lay my head.

THE SONG OF THE BLINDMAN

I am blind, you out there -- that is a curse,
against one's will, a contradiction,
a heavy daily burden.
I lay my hand on the arm of my wife,
my grey hand upon her greyer grey,
as she guides me through empty spaces.

You move about and stir, and imagine
your sounds differing from stone on stone.
But you are mistaken: I alone
live and suffer and complain, for
in me is an endless crying,
and I do not know whether it is
my heart that cries or my bowels.

Do you recognize these songs? You never sang them,
not quite with this intonation.
For you every morning brings its new light
warm through your open windows.
And you have the feeling from face to face
that tempts you to be indulgent.

THE SONG OF THE DRUNKARD

It was not in me. It moved in and out.
When I dared to stop it, the wine won out.
(What it was, I no longer remember.)
The wine then offered this and offered that,
till I became dependent upon him,
I, fool!

Now I am part of his game, as he throws me
around in utter contempt, and surely he will
lose me this day to that scavenger: death.
When death wins me, soiled card that I am,
he will use me only to scratch his sordid scabs
and toss me away into the mire.

THE SONG OF THE SUICIDE

*W*ell then, one final look around.
How they have always managed to cut
my rope!
Lately I was so well prepared
that in my entrails I sensed already
something of eternity.

They keep on offering me the spoon:
this spoon containing life.
No, I want none of it, not now or ever,
let me go and vomit . . . . .

I know that life is altogether good,
the world itself a brimful pot,
but my blood refuses to absorb it,
instead it goes right to my head.

What nourishes others makes me sick.
Do realize that I scorn life.
For at least a thousand years to come
I will have to diet.

THE SONG OF THE WIDOW

*I*n the beginning life was good to me;
it held me warm and gave me courage.
That this is granted all while in their youth,
how could I then have known of this.
I never knew what living was ----.
But suddenly it was just year on year,
no more good, no more new, no more wonderful.
Life had been torn in two right down the middle.

That was not his fault nor mine
since both of us had nothing but patience;
but death has none.
I saw him coming (how rotten he looked),
and I watched him as he took and took:
and nothing was mine.

What, then, belonged to me; was mine, my own?
Was not even this utter wretchedness
on loan to me by fate?
Fate does not only claim your happiness,
it also wants your pain back and your tears
and buys the ruin as something useless, old.

Fate was present and acquired for a nothing
every expression my face is capable of,
even to the way I walk.
The daily diminishing of me went on
and after I was emptied fate gave me up
and left me standing there, abandoned.

THE SONG OF THE IDIOT

They do not hinder me. They let me go.
They say, nothing could happen.
How good.
Nothing can happen. Everything comes and circles
uninterrupted around the Holy Ghost,
around that certain ghost (you know) --,
how good.

No, one really must never think that there
could be any danger involved in this.
There is, of course, the blood.
Blood is the heaviest. For blood is heavy.
Sometimes I believe, I can no longer -----.
How good.

Ah, what a lovely ball that is:
red and round all over.
Good that you brought it.
I wonder would it come if I called?

How odd everything behaves,
driving into each other, swimming away from each other:
friendly, though a little confused:
how good.

THE SONG OF THE ORPHAN

I am no one and never will be anyone,
for I am far too small to claim to be;
not even later.

Mothers and Fathers,
take pity on me.

I fear it will not pay to raise me:
I shall fall victim to the mower's scythe.
No one can find me useful now: I am too young,
and tomorrow will be too late.

I only have one dress,
worn thin and faded,
but it will last an eternity
even before God, perhaps.

I only have this whispy hair
(that always remained the same)
yet once was someone's dearest love.

Now he has nothing that he loves.

THE SONG OF THE DWARF

Perhaps my soul is straight and sound;
but my heart, my warped blood,
everything that causes me pain,
my soul cannot carry erect.
It has no garden, it has no bed,
it hangs and pulls on my sharp skeleton
with beating wings that terrify.

As for my hands, they never will change shape.
Look here how they are stunted in their growth,
stubbornly they hop about, damp and heavy,
like little toads leaping after rain.
See how the rest of me is worn,
old and sad;
why does God hesitate to throw away
all this on the nearest dungheap?

Is it because my poor face angers Him
with its sullen mouth?
It was so many times prepared to smile,
bright and clear throughout its contours:
but nothing ever came so close to Him
as those enormous dogs.
And dogs do not have such problems.

THE SONG OF THE LEPER

See, I am one everyone has deserted.
No one in the city knows of me.
I have fallen victim to leprosy.
I beat my wooden clappers and knock
the pitiable sight of me
into the ears of everyone
that passes near me.
And those who hear the wooden sound
avert their eyes, look elsewhere,
not wanting to know what has befallen me.

Where the sound of my rattle reaches,
I am at home; perhaps it is you
who makes it sound so loud, that no one
dares to be too far from me
who now avoids to come too close to me.
So now I can walk for ever so long
without encountering a girl, a woman or man,
or even a child.

Animals I do not frighten.

END POEM

*D*eath is immense.
We all are his
with laughing mouths.
When we are in
the midst of life
he dares to weep
right in our midst.

FROM THE TWO BOOKS

of

NEW POEMS

(NEUE GEDICHTE)

1907 and 1908

ARCHAIC TORSO OF APOLLO

(A mon grand Ami Auguste Rodin)

*L*ost is for us the sun god's glorious head
which held the eyes' unfathomable gaze,
but like a miracle, turning his glance
inward, incandescent his torso gleams

and casts a spell. How else could light pour forth
across the breast's expanse and blind you with
its grace? And softly now descend the curve,
caressing with a smile the thighs
that cradle man's renewing source of life.

Else would this marble torso stand defaced
and short beneath the shoulders' broad expanse,
and would not glisten like a wild beast's fur,

nor would its contours burst forth like a star.
For every part of this commanding form
holds you in its gaze. Henceforth your life must change.

EARLY APOLLO

*A*s when sometimes through branches, leafless still,
a morning bursts with all the force of Spring,
so there is nothing in his head that could
prevent the radiant power of all poems

to strike us almost deadly with its light.
For there is yet no shadow in his gaze,
too cool for laurel are his temples still,
and round the eyebrows only later will

come climbing long-stemmed roses from his garden,
and petals, separating from their blooms,
will drift and rest upon his trembling mouth

that yet is silent, sparkling and unused,
and only hinting with a smile as if
a song were soon to reach his open lips.

ROMAN FOUNTAIN

(Villa Borghese, Rome)

Two basins,
one above the other suspended
and both upheld
over the ancient marble pool below,
the water gently rising and falling,
reaching the brim and gliding
down to the waiting basin below
that like an upheld mirror
reflecting sky and clouds
hiding behind dark evergreens
objects indistinguishable,
dreamlike continuing on its course,
without regret,
circle upon circle,
till lazily reaching the moss-clad rim
and surrendering to its final mirror,
drop by drop,
causing the pool to smile darkly from below,
rippling by its overflowing.

SONG OF THE SEA

(Capri, Piccola Marina)

*T*imeless sea breezes,
sea-wind of the night:
you come for no one;
if someone should wake,
he must be prepared
how to survive you.

Timeless sea breezes,
that for aeons have
blown on ancient rocks,
you are purest space
coming from afar ...

Oh, how a fruit-bearing
fig tree feels your coming
high up in the moonlight.

CATHEDRAL OF SAINT MARK

(Venice)

*W*ithin this inner space, that seems as if
it had been hollowed out, suggested by the
arches curving upward supporting golden
vaults, round-edged, smooth, niches filled with preciousness:

within this space was kept in darkness the city's
treasures, secretly collected, as a counterweight
to the light, that in all things multiplied itself
so rapidly, that they almost seemed to disappear ---,

and suddenly you feel impelled to doubt:
will they remain? And you push your way through
the gallery that, like a catwalk in a gold mine hangs
near the shining arches of the ceiling; and you

are relieved to find yourself standing in the
brilliant light shining through the windows
above the team of the four famous horses of antiquity,
while you cast regretful glances backward as you leave.

THE APPLE ORCHARD

*C*ome let us watch the sun go down
and walk in twilight through the orchard's green.
Does it not seem as if we had for long
collected, saved and harbored within us
old memories? To find release and seek
new hopes, remembering half-forgotten joys,
mingled with darkness coming from within,
as we randomly voice our thoughts aloud
wandering beneath these harvest-laden trees
reminiscent of Dürer woodcuts, branches
which, bent under the fully ripened fruit,
wait patiently, trying to outlast, to
serve another season's hundred days of toil,
straining, uncomplaining, by not breaking
but succeeding, even though the burden
should at times seem almost past endurance.
Not to falter! Not to be found wanting!

Thus must it be, when willingly you strive
throughout a long and uncomplaining life,
committed to one goal: to give yourself!
And silently to grow and to bear fruit.

SELF-PORTRAIT

(from the year 1906)

*T*he steadfastness of generations of nobility
shows in the curving lines that form the eyebrows.
And the blue eyes still show traces of childhood fears
and of humility here and there, not of a servant's,
yet of one who serves obediently, and of a woman.
The mouth formed as a mouth, large and accurate,
not given to long phrases, but to express
persuasively what is right. The forehead without guile
and favoring the shadows of quiet downward gazing.

This, as a coherent whole, only casually observed;
never as yet tried in suffering or succeeding,
held together for an enduring fulfillment,
yet so as if for times to come, out of these scattered things,
something serious and lasting were being planned.

LOVE SONG

*H*ow shall I hold my soul suspended above you
so that it does not touch on yours? How shall
I succeed in concentrating on other things?
Oh, gladly would I hide my soul with something lost,
somewhere in darkness in a totally strange place
that would prevent my soul's vibrating, when yours
vibrates in all its depths.

But everything that touches you and me
takes us together, like the player's bow
who out of two strings creates one melody.

Upon which instrument are we then strung?
Whose is the master-hand that holds the bow?

O sweet song ....

SLUMBER SONG

Some day, if I should ever lose you,
will you be able then to go to sleep
without me softly whispering above you
like night air stirring in the linden tree?

Without my waking here and watching
and saying words as tender as eyelids
that come to rest weightlessly upon your breast,
upon your sleeping limbs, upon your lips?

Without my touching you and leaving you
alone with what is yours, like a summer garden
that is overflowing with masses
of melissa and star-anise?

ADAM

(Rheims Cathedral, 1908)

*H*igh above he stands, beside the many
saintly figures fronting the cathedral's
gothic tympanum, close by the window
called the rose, and looks astonished at his

own deification which placed him there.
Erect and proud he smiles, and quite enjoys
this feat of his survival, willed by choice.

As labourer in the fields he made his start
and through his efforts brought to full fruition
the garden God named Eden. But where was
the hidden path that led to the New Earth?

God would not listen to his endless pleas.
Instead, He threatened him that he shall die.
Yet Adam stood his ground: Eve shall give birth.

EVE

(Rheims Cathedral, 1908)

*L*ook how she stands, high on the steep facade
of the cathedral, near the window-rose,
simply, holding in her hand the apple,
judged for all time as the guiltless-guilty

for the growing fruit her body held
which she gave birth to after parting from
the circle of eternities. She left
to face the strange New Earth, so young in years.

Oh, how she would have loved to stay a little
longer in that enchanted garden, where
the peaceful gentle beasts grazed side by side.

But Adam was resolved to leave, to go
out into this New Earth, and facing death
she followed him. God she had hardly known.

SAINT GEORGE

*A*nd so she called for him throughout the night
upon her knees, this frail exhausted maid:
Can you not see the dragon in his lair?
Why does he keep his guard, awake, alert?

Then through the morning's pale-grey mist he came
on dappled horse, his face and armour shining.
He found her kneeling as she upward looked,
enraptured at the radiance that was his.

And off he rode full speed across the land,
as downwards, with his lance held high and steady
within both hands, he faced the open danger,
proud of the challenge that he chose to meet.

But she kept on beseeching, kneeling more
intensely, praying now more fervently
with hands still tighter clasped: he must succeed!
For she knew not that victory would come to *him*

for whom she offered up her pure and ready heart.
Then hosts of heavenly messengers clothed in light
encircled him for combat. By his side
stood, strong as towers stand, her prayer.

SAINT SEBASTIAN

*A*s one recumbent, so he stands
totally upheld by his great will.
Withdrawn as mothers are when suckling still,
and wrapt within himself as by a wreath.

The arrows fly: up, up they come
as if they sprang from out his tender loins,
each iron quivering along its end.
Yet he smiles darkly and remains unhurt.

Once only, oh, so great his sorrow grows,
his eyes reveal the pain as he looks on,
but they change to denial, judging those
inferior as they scornfully let go
the vile destroyers of a lovely thing.

THE GAZELLE

(Jardin des Plantes, Paris)

*E*nchanted one: how can the unison of two
selected words ever attain the rhythm
which in you comes and goes as if by signal.
Out of your forehead leaf and lyre rise,

and all your being in comparison
moves through our love songs, as their words, soft as
rose petals resting upon the eyelids
of him who stopped reading to observe you

with half-closed eyes, you standing there as though
your limbs with leaps were charged but not released
as long as your so slender neck held still

supporting the listening head: as when a maiden,
interrupted in her bathing, turns quickly,
reflecting in her eyes the forest lake.

THE FLAMINGOS

(Paris, Jardin des Plantes)

*L*ike mirror-images of canvases by Fragonard -
reflecting shimmering hues of white and red -
they offer you no more than if a friend said casually
of his love: "She was still sleeping softly."

They step from water basin to the island's green,
high on their stilt-like rosy legs, to gather -
resembling more a flowering bed of blossoms -
as they seductively hold court, more cunningly than Phryne,

until, with pallid eyes, their slender necks and beaks
seek refuge, hiding deep within their downy wings,
where tints of black hide with the red of ripened fruit.

Quite suddenly the air is pierced by shrieks of jealousy;
they only stretch themselves and look astonished
as they stride singly past into the imaginary.

THE SWAN

*T*his toiling labor for a goal not yet achieved
that like a heavy burden hinders every step,
is like the swan's ungainly awkward gait

which illuminates this dying, this no longer
holding on to the ground on which we daily stand,
so like his anxious lowering of himself --:

into the waters that receive him gently,
and then, happy and bygone, begin to lift him
wave to wave, receding soundlessly beneath him,
while he, infinitely still and self-assured
and ever more mature, with regal bearing,
deigns to be borne serenely drifting by.

THE BULLFIGHT

(Corrida)

*H*e seemed surprisingly small as he broke out of the
opened bull pen. With startled eyes and ears alert,
he viewed his baiting attackers with their beribboned
banderillas as part of a game. Then suddenly

he changed into the formidable animal that he was, --
see: his massiveness filled with an old black hate
as his lowered head takes on the shape of a clenched fist.
He no longer plays games with anyone.

Oh no! The bloody steel-spiked lances of the
picadors sink in behind the lowered horns into his
back, as enraged he faces the matador,
his opponent destined since eternity,

who in his gold and mauve-rose costume
suddenly turns round, and, like a swarm of bees,
as if completely at ease, he casually lets
the storming beast pass beneath his outstretched arm,

while his burning eyes look upward to the stands,
surveying calmly the throng surrounding the arena,
as if with every opening and closing of his eyes
the crowds drifted down to him in light and shade,

till he quite calm, unhating, leaning on himself,
relaxed, nonchalant meets the final assault,
the mounting wave that loses as it strikes, so that
his sword sinks almost softly into the dying bull.

SPANISH DANCER

*A*s in one's hand a lighted match blinds you before
it comes aflame and sends out brilliant flickering
tongues to every side -- so, within the ring of the
spectators, her dance begins in hasty, heated rhythms
and spreads itself like darting flames around.

And suddenly the dance is altogether flame!

With a fierce glance she sets her hair alight.
Unexpectedly she turns with daring artfulness
the swirling flounces of her dress within this
conflagration, out of which her upheld naked arms,
clapping the castanets, appear like serpents striking.

And then, afraid her fire were diminishing,
she gathers it all up and flings it down
with an imperious haughty gesture, and watches
as it lies there writhing on the ground, unyielding
and unwilling to concede the dance has ended.
Yet she shows victory in her sweet swift smile
as she lifts up her face, while with her small firm feet
she stamps out the last of the dying embers.

THE PANTHER

(Jardin des Plantes, Paris.)

*H*is tired gaze - from passing endless bars -
has turned into a vacant stare which nothing holds.
To him there seem to be a thousand bars,
and out beyond these bars exists no world.

His supple gait, the smoothness of strong strides
that gently turn in ever smaller circles
perform a dance of strength, centered deep within
a will, stunned, but untamed, indomitable.

But sometimes the curtains of his eyelids part,
the pupils of his eyes dilate as images
of past encounters enter while through his limbs
a tension strains in silence
only to cease to be, to die within his heart.

OVERWHELM ME, MUSIC

*O*verwhelm me, Music, with your rhythmic raging!
High reproach, held close up to the heart
that wavered in responding to you fully, sparing itself.
                    My heart: *there:*
behold your glory. Are you more often content
to vibrate less? But these vaultings, the uppermost,
wait for you to fill them with the organ's pulsing sound.
Why do you long to see the withdrawn countenance
                    of your absent beloved?
Does not your yearning have breath, like the
                    Angel's trumpet announcing
the Last Judgment, to sound piercingly through storms:
oh, she *is* nowhere, does not exist, will not be born,
of whom you are deprived, slowly fading away ...

ON HEARING OF A DEATH

*W*e lack all knowledge of this parting. Death
does not deal with us. We have no reason
to show death admiration, love or hate;
his mask of feigned tragic lament gives us

a false impression. The world's stage is still
filled with roles which we play. While we worry
that our performances may not please,
death also performs, although to no applause.

But as you left us, there broke upon this stage
a glimpse of reality, shown through the slight
opening through which you disappeared: green,
evergreen, bathed in sunlight, actual woods.

We keep on playing, still anxious, our difficult roles
declaiming, accompanied by matching gestures
as required. But your presence so suddenly
removed from our midst and from our play, at times

overcomes us like a sense of that other
reality: yours, that we are so overwhelmed
and play our actual lives instead of the performance,
forgetting altogether the applause.

THE UNICORN

*T*he saintly hermit, midway through his prayers
stopped suddenly, and raised his eyes to witness
the unbelievable: for there before him stood
the legendary creature, startling white, that
had approached, soundlessly, pleading with his eyes.

The legs, so delicately shaped, balanced a
body wrought of finest ivory. And as
he moved, his coat shone like reflected moonlight.
High on his forehead rose the magic horn, the sign
of his uniqueness: a tower held upright
by his alert, yet gentle, timid gait.

The mouth of softest tints of rose and grey, when
opened slightly, revealed his gleaming teeth,
whiter than snow. The nostrils quivered faintly:
he sought to quench his thirst, to rest and find repose.
His eyes looked far beyond the saint's enclosure,
reflecting vistas and events long vanished,
and closed the circle of this ancient mystic legend.

THE MERRY-GO-ROUND

(Jardin du Luxembourg)

*U*nder its roof that casts a cooling shadow
the carousel keeps circling for a while
with brightly painted horses, all from the land
that lingers long before it disappears.
Though some of them are pulling carriages,
still all show pride and boldness in their mien;
a vicious-looking lion, all in red, goes with them,
and now and then appears a snow-white elephant.

Even a stag is there, just as in woodlands,
save that he wears a saddle on which rides
a little girl in blue, securely buckled.

Upon the lion's back a boy in white
rides, holding anxiously onto the reins,
while fierce the lion shows his teeth and tongue.

And now and then appears a snow-white elephant.

And on their horses they come charging by,
among them girls who almost have outgrown
this galloping of steeds; midway in passing
they look about, across, up, over, anywhere ---

And now and then appears a snow-white elephant.

And so it circles round and hurries on toward
the finish, always turning, for it has no goal.
A red, a green, a grey keep flying past us --
a little profile comes and is already gone.
At times a smile comes floating by, for us
intended, a blissful happy smile, lightly
expended upon this blind and breathless game.

THE ANGEL OF THE MERIDIAN

(Chartres Cathedral)

*A*midst the storm that round the great cathedral
rages like an atheist who thinks and thinks,
we suddenly are drawn with tender feelings
toward your smiling countenance among the saints.

Beguiling angel, sympathetic statue,
with mouth as fashioned from a hundred mouths:
are you aware how from your full sundial
our hours keep gliding past into oblivion

as do our days like a procession, measured
equally by your dial's impartial balancing,
as if each hour and day had reached full ripeness.

What do you know, stone angel, of our being?
And does your blessed face increase in radiance
as you uphold the sundial out into the night?

THE RAISING OF LAZARUS

*I*t seemed, in order to convince those doubting him,
he must give signs of his inherent power that shouted!
But he was dreaming when he thought he need not prove
himself to Martha and Mary: he felt they knew
he *could!* Instead, no one believed him. For all spoke out:
Lord, wherefore didst thou come *now?*
He then decided to do the impermissible:
to act against the fundamental laws of nature.
Filled with anger, with eyes half closed, he demanded
to be shown the grave. He suffered. And they witnessed
his flowing tears as they around him crowded, --
more out of curiosity than compassion.

While he walked toward the grave he shuddered at the thought
of this monstrous, horrible playing experiment.
But suddenly an uncontrollable, all-consuming
fire broke out within him, a contradiction
against all their differences, their being dead,
their being alive, that he felt a hatred
invading every limb as he commanded them:
Remove the stone!

A voice warned him that the body already smelled, ---
(for he had lain buried for the fourth day) --- but He
stood taut, erect, completely controlled by that call
which rose within him and raised his heavy, o so heavy
hand ---(Never before had such a hand been raised
so slowly and with such an enormous effort) ---
until his arm stood upright, shining in the sun,
while high above the hand changed into an open claw!

For now he was seized by horror, as if all the dead
might take the signal from the opened grave and rise
together with the body that rose up with effort, --
pale, partly decomposed -- from its lying position.
But then there stood up only *One*, obliquely,
in the light of day, and all there saw it happen:
the indistinct, vague *Life* returning to him
and granting the reprieve.

GETHSEMANE

(The Garden of Olives)

*H*e climbed upward beneath the greying foliage
of the garden's olive trees, merging with them
as he laid his forehead full of dust into
his even more dust-covered burning hands.

After all, this! And this, then, meant the end. --
Now I am to leave while I am going blind.
And why do you insist that I must say: *you are*,
when I myself no longer can find you?

No longer can I find you. Not within me, no.
And not in others. Not even in this stone.
I find you never more. I am alone.

I am alone with all of mankind's sorrow
which I through you to ease and lighten undertook,
you whom I no longer find. O nameless shame . . . .

Later, so it was told: an angel came. --

Wherefore an angel? Oh, the night descended
and played among the foliage of the trees.
The sleeping disciples stirred within their dreams.
Wherefore an angel? Oh, the night had come.

The night that came was not one called uncommon:
thus pass a hundred nights without concern.
There dogs lie sleeping, and stones lie dormant.
Another sad night, any one of many
that wait until it is morning once again.

For angels do not answer such men's prayers,
and nights do not surround such men with greatness.
Those who are lost within themselves all things forsake.
They are abandoned, cast out by their fathers,
and are expulsed even from their mother's womb.

CRUCIFIXION

*A*s executioners they had long learned to handle
the curious crowds that always followed them
whenever they were on their way to Golgotha,
the barren mount of gallows. Now and then they jeeringly

looked backward at the following three condemned.
But once arrived they made short shrift of them
and having finished with their gruesome job, they
turned to leave since all they had to do was done.

Until one in the crowd - a sleezy character -
shouted: Captain, this one has called out aloud!
And seated on his horse the captain asked: which one?
It seemed to him as if he, too, had heard him call

Elijah! The rabble now stirred and gathered gaping
around the caller. And to make certain that he
stayed alive, they held up to his lips the sponge
soaked full of vinegar to stop his rasping cough.

They hoped that by continuing to taunt him
this game may still produce the coming of Elijah . . . .
But far behind the mob there cried the Mother
of Him who now let out a terrible scream and died.

CHRIST AND THE DISCIPLES AT EMMAUS

*N*ot yet by his gait, although strangely assured
he walked toward them, ready to join them on their way;
and though he stepped across the dwelling's threshold
more solemn than they did in their manliness;
not yet, as they chose places round the table,
placing upon it a simple fare of this and that,
and he, at ease, relaxed, unhurriedly let rest
upon them his observing eyes;
not even now, as they were seated and hospitably
began to get acquainted with each other,
and he reached for the bread with his beautiful
hesitating hands, proceeding to break the loave,
that they -- like sudden shock affects an unsuspecting crowd --
were overwhelmed with fear and with tremendous awe -------
For now, at last, with eyesight clearing, as he
dispelled the tension in the room by offering:
they recognized him! And shaken, jumping to their feet,
stood there, bent, and filled with anxious love.

Then, as they saw him staying, hands outstretched in giving,
they tremblingly reached for the offered bread.

THE LIFE OF THE VIRGIN MARY

(DAS MARIENLEBEN)

(1912)

THE BIRTH OF MARY

*O*h, what restraint it must have cost the angels
not to burst suddenly into song, as one bursts into tears,
because of their knowing: that this very night
will witness the birth of the Mother, she who is destined
to bring forth the son, the Saviour, who shall appear.

Soaring aloft together they silently pointed the way
where, hidden and isolated, the farm of Joachim lay.
Oh, how they felt within and around them the mounting tension,
so great, they longed to attend! But none was allowed to descend.

Since by this time both were exhausted from making preparations.
A neighbor's wife came by and was full of suggestions, but proved
of little help, while aged Joachim, cautiously, entered
the darkened stable to calm a restless cow from mooing . . . .
For there had never been a night like this!

THE PRESENTATION OF MARY IN THE TEMPLE

*T*o comprehend what she herself felt at the time,
you must in your imagination place yourself
somewhere where pillars rise and columns work in you;
where you anticipate the feel of rising steps;
where arches dangerously bridge the chasm
of a space that stayed in you, because you failed
to stop the piling up of broken pieces,
which you no longer now can extricate from
within you, without risking your total collapse.

When you shall have succeeded - when all in you
is stone, wall, stairway, vaulting, vista - then with both
hands try to pull slightly aside the heavy curtain
that separates you and there before you hangs:

Then shall you see the radiance of imposing objects,
totally overpowering your breath and senses.
And looking up and down before you, you will observe
palace upon palace, balustrades streaming out of
balustrades that reappear high above on ledges,
so that you, from looking up at them, become quite dizzy.

Pale smoke rising from nearby incense burners
cloud your vision, while from the farthest distance
rays of brilliant light pierce through to you ---,
and added to this is the shimmering light from
transluscent bowls of flames that play upon the dazzling
raiments of priests slowly advancing in procession ---:
How can you survive all this splendor?

But she arrived and lifted up her eyes
to witness and absorb all of this happening.
(A child, a maiden, accompanied by women.)
Then she began quietly, full of self-confidence,
to climb the steps ahead, toward the pomp and ceremony
that fastidiously moved aside for her to pass:
So much was all that mankind ever built
already outweighed by the praise within

her heart. By her intense desire
to offer herself up to all the inner signs:
The parents thought they were delivering her
up to the threatening one with the bejeweled
breast plate who seemingly received her.
Yet she walked through them all -- little as she was --
forth out of every hand and into her destiny,
which, higher than the hall, was all in readiness,
and heavier than the temple.

THE ANNUNCIATION

*N*ot that an angel entering her room
(remember) was the cause that startled her.
She gave no further thought to an angel's
appearance as others notice beams of
sunlight, or that of the moon at night, play
hide and seek upon the walls and ceiling
of their chambers. And that these journeys were
quite troublesome for angels never crossed her mind.

(Oh, if we only knew how pure she was!
Did not a doe, that resting, once espied
her in the woods so lose herself in looking
that in her, without pairing, the unicorn
begot itself, the animal of light, the creature pure --.)

Not that the angel's entrance was the cause,
but his youthful face bending so closely
above hers, that, when looking up, her eyes
met his, so powerfully, as though the world
outside were suddenly all emptied, and
what many millions saw, pursued and carried
were crowded into them: angel and maid;
seeing, and that which is seen: eye and eye's delight,
and nowhere else save in this chamber --: see,
this is startling! And they were startled, both.

The angel then began his joyful song.

VISITATION OF THE VIRGIN

*H*er life at first continued on its gentle course.
Only when climbing were there times when she
became aware of her wondrous body's changing, --
then she stood, catching her breath, upon the high hills

of Judea. But it was not the land she saw:
it was her own abundance which spread about her;
and as she went she felt that no one ever could
exceed the greatness which she felt within herself.

She had a longing just to lay her hand
upon the other's body, which was further on.
And as both women swayed toward each other
they touched their bodies, garments and their hair.

Each woman, quite aware of her holy fullness,
sought comfort and protection from her kin.
Oh, the Saviour in her womb was still a flower,
while in her cousin's body the Baptist began
to leap for joy in exultation.

JOSEPH'S SUSPICION

The angel spoke and patiently tried to
convince the man, who met him with clenched fists:
Can you not see that in her every way
she is as cool as God's first morning mist?

And yet the man looked at him glowering with
suspicion, murmuring: what has brought about her change?
But then the angel cried in anger: Carpenter!
Do you not yet perceive the hand of God's own doing?

Because you handle wood and know your trade,
do you in arrogance call Him to task
who from the self-same wood you handle now
can make green leaves appear and swelling buds?

He understood. And as he raised his eyes,
now full of fear, to meet the angel's face,
he was gone. Slowly Joseph removed his cap.
Then he began to sing his song of praise.

ANNUNCIATION ABOVE THE SHEPHERDS

*L*ook up, you shepherds! You men there round the fire!
You who possess the ancient knowledge of the
boundless heavens and read the stars, look here! See,
I am a new and rising star. My entire being
burns and shines so strongly, and is so immensely
full of light, that the far-flung firmament can
no longer hold me. Let my radiance enter
into your existence: Oh, the dark looks, the dark hearts,
the darker destinies that fill you now!
Shepherds, how alone am I in you. All of
a sudden I find room. Were you not astonished when
the spreading breadfruit tree threw a deep shadow?
Yes, that came from me. You fearless ones; oh, if
you knew how now upon your shining faces
the future is illuminated. In this strong light
so much will happen. In you I can confide,
for I can trust you well to be discreet;
to you humble believers all things here speak:
heat and rainfall speak; so does the flight of birds,
the wind and what you are; for nothing outweighs
the other nor develops into vanity and gluttony.

You do not hold things hostage imprisoned in your
breast so to torment them. Just as an angel
contemplates in ecstasy, so does the earthly life
course through your veins. And should there suddenly
appear before you a burning bush, and from its center
you could hear the Lord God's voice addressing you;
Or if a cherubim decided to gently walk alongside
your grazing flocks; all this would not surprise you:
for you would prostate yourselves and fall upon your faces,
worshipping God and calling this the earth.

Yet this was then. Now shall a new beginning
cause the earth to expand in ever wider circles.
What for us is a burning bush, is:
God in His unfathomable wisdom has chosen
to bless a virgin's womb.
I am the light that points the way to her.
Come, follow me!

THE BIRTH OF CHRIST

*W*ere you not blessed with such humility,
this miracle of birth would not have come to us through you
that now lights up the night a thousandfold.

See how Our Lord - whose laws have kept mankind
bowed down in utter fear and awe - now shows
to us an image of such tenderness
as He descends into our world through you.

Had you a greater vision in your mind of Him before?
How can one fathom greatness?

Suspending momentarily the laws that govern life
He headed straight toward His chosen goal.
Not even stars, predestined in their course,
can alter their celestial destinies and paths.

Do you observe three kings advancing toward you?
They are of noble birth and heap before your feet
such treasures which they value as their greatest.
Are you, perhaps, astonished at these gifts?

But look! Behold! For there upon your lap,
wrapped lovingly in swaddling clothes, lies He
who even now outshines in dazzling brilliance
these treasures which the Magi hither brought:

the amber which ships carried from afar,
the ornaments of gold and precious jewels,
the aromatic spices, foremost myrrh,
with which to sanctify the air with burning incense.

The kings departed, and their royal gifts
were yours for just a short duration.
(Did someone sense the loss and feel regret?)
But you will live to see: He brings enduring joy!

REST ON THE FLIGHT TO EGYPT

*T*hey did escape! Breathlessly fleeing from the midst
of the ruthless slaughter of innocent children.
Oh, how they had aged unknowingly from facing
the dangers along their perilous wandering.

Yet, taking a timid backward look to see if they
had bypassed other dangers, so they could relax:
they faced new problems, as on their gray mule they entered
and caused whole cities to tremble with fear, for,

little as they were - an almost nothing -
when nearing the temples of this ancient land,
all their idols exploded as if by betrayal,
utterly losing their composure and their senses.

Is it conceivable that at their passing
all things became so desparately enraged?
They even were becoming afraid of themselves.
Only the child remained supremely at ease!

After this - and for the moment safe - they felt the need
to finally rest awhile. But there -- see: looking up,
the tree that overshadowed them in silence,
bent over them as if to say: I am your servant;

and it bowed as if to pay obeisance. For it was
this tree that grew the garland-fashioned crowns
which adorned the brows of long departed Pharaohs.
And suddenly it felt new crowns burst into flower.

They sat and rested, as if in a dream.

OF THE MARRIAGE AT CANA

*C*ould she be otherwise than proud of him
who turned to beauty the simplest of her gestures?
Was not even the night that spans the universe
beside itself with joy when he was born?

Did he not also - having lost his way -
once find himself the center of unheard-of praise?
Had not the wisest men exchanged their mouths
for ears? Did not the temple suddenly seem new

after listening to his clear and learned voice?
Oh, there had been hundreds of occasions when she
restrained herself from radiantly sharing
her joy of him with others. In awe she followed him.

It happened at the wedding feast at Cana,
when unexpectedly the hosts ran out of wine --
she sought his eyes and pleaded for a gesture,
but could not comprehend why he declined.

And then he acted! Later on she understood
how she had, without thinking, forced him in his way:
for now he really was performing miracles,
and in his future loomed the sacrifice he was

to suffer, irrevocably. Yes, so it had been written.
But was it even then in preparation?
She: she had in the blindness of her vanity
set into motion the force of his destruction.

Seated at the table's abundance of fruit
and vegetables, she rejoiced with others,
not knowing that the water of her tear-glands
had turned to blood within the flowing wine.

BEFORE THE PASSION

*O*h, if this was your will, you should not have come forth
out of the softness of a woman's body.
Saviours should come from mountain quarries
where from the hardest core one breaks the hardest rock.

Do you not feel regret for having devastated
the valley you once loved? Look at my weakness;
I have no more to give than flowing milk and tears,
and you were always first in my affection.

With what exalted honors were you promised me!
Why did you not at once force yourself out of me?
If you need only tigers to tear you limb from limb,
why did they have to raise me in the women's house

to weave for you a cloak of softest wool
in which not even traces of a seam could press
against your body? --: my whole life was like that!
And now you suddenly reversed all nature's course.

PIETÀ

*N*ow is my suffering complete as pain
unutterable fills my entire being.
I stare, am numb and rigid as a rock
is rigid to its very core.

Hard as I am, I do remember this:
You grew to boyhood ---
. . . grew in height and strength,
you stood apart and overshadowed me,
became too great a sorrow, far beyond
the limits of my poor heart's understanding.

Now you lie, stilled in death, across my lap;
now I no longer can bring back your life
through birth.

CONSOLATION OF MARY WITH THE RISEN CHRIST

*W*hat at that moment they experienced:
was it not sweet still in its undisclosed
secret as the earthly event it was:
as He, still somewhat pale from lying in
the grave, stepped toward her, seemingly relieved:
His resurrection shone from all His being.

Oh, to her first! How were they then both healed
inexpressibly by its soothing action.
Yes, they were healing, that was happening.
They had no need to firmly touch each other.
He laid for hardly a second His soon to be
eternal hand upon her motherly shoulder.

And they began - still as the trees in spring -
infinitely close, this season of their
eternally enduring communion.

OF THE DEATH OF MARY

(Part I)

*I*t was the same great angel who had once before
appeared to her, bringing her the message of her bearing.
He stood there quietly waiting for her to recognize him,
then spoke: Now has the time arrived for you to appear.
And she was startled just as she was then,
and was once more the maiden, deeply confirming him.
But he shone, and infinitely near to her
became as one within her face -- and bode
the widely dispersed evangelists to come together
here in the small house upon the slope,
the house of the Last Supper.
They came more weighted down and entered fearfully:

There, upon the narrow bed, lay she,
mysteriously immersed in thoughts of leaving
and making decisions of selection, so well preserved
as of one never used, and seemingly absorbed
in listening to a choir of angels singing.

Now that she saw them all, gathered behind
their lighted candles, she tore herself away
from the exalted voices, and made a present
with all her heart of her two remaining robes
that she possessed, lifting her face up now to this one,
now to that......
(O source of countless streams of flowing tears!)

But she lay back, and in her weakness drew the heavens
so close down to Jerusalem, so near, that her departing
soul need only to stretch itself a little:
And he, who everything about her knew, lifted her up
into her divine nature.

(Part II)

*W*ho had ever thought that until her arrival
the immense heaven had remained incomplete?
Her resurrected son had occupied His throne,
but next to Him, throughout twenty-four years,
the seat remained unused. Already they began
to take the empty space for granted that appeared
to be reserved, for her son in His luminescence
filled her place with light to overflowing.

She, therefore, did not go to Him directly
as she entered into heaven, much as she desired.
She could see no vacant place, only He was there,
resplendent with a radiance that pained her.
Yet as she now - this, oh, so touching figure -
joined inconspicuously the ranks of all the
newly blessed - light and transparent - as she stood,
there shone out of her being a hidden reserve
of such brilliance that the angel next to her,
blinded by her light, cried out: Who is she?

All were astonished. Then they witnessed how
high above God the Father withdrew our Lord
so that his powerful light shining upon the
empty place was reduced to twilight, making it
appear somewhat sad, lonely, like something being
still endured, a remainder of earthly suffering ---.

All looked at her: she looked out, timidly,
bending far forward as if feeling: I am His most
enduring pain ---: and suddenly she collapsed.
But the angels, lifting her up, took her to themselves,
supporting her as they sang ecstatically,
and carried her at last to her appointed place.

(Part III)

    *T*hen in front of Thomas the Apostle - who arrived just
when it was too late - stepped swiftly the angel
who was quite prepared for this event and took command
at the burial-place.

Come, and push the stone aside! Would you like
to know where she is now that so moved your heart:
See: she was laid down for a little while inside
like a pillow filled with dried blossoms of lavender

so that in future the earth might carry
the sweet scent of her in its folds like a fine cloth.
All things dead (you sense) and all things decaying
are overcome and soothed by her aromatic fragrance.

Behold the winding-sheet: Where is there a place
for bleaching so that it would remain dazzlingly white
and unshrunk? But the light that emanated from her
pure corpse proved far more clarifying than the sun.

And did it not astonish you, how gently she left it?
Almost as though it were still she, nothing having changed.
Yet the heavens high above are trembling:
Man, fall on your knees, watch my departure, and sing!

SONNETS TO ORPHEUS

(SONNETTE AN ORPHEUS)

(1922)

SONNETS TO ORPHEUS

(Book I, #1)

*T*here rose a tree. O magic transcendence!
Orpheus sings! And in the ear a tree!
Silence reigned. Yet even in this silence
a new beginning dawned and changes came.

For creatures stepped soundlessly from clearings
of forests and left lair and nest behind;
and all this happened not through fear or fright
that made them so intent on keeping still:

the better to listen. Howling, crying,
roaring seemed small within their hearts. And where
there was scarcely a hut to shelter them,—

a hiding place out of their darkest longings,
with an entrance gate whose structure trembled,—
there you created temples in their ears!

SONNETS TO ORPHEUS

(Book I, #4)

O gentle lovers, forego not to step
into the breath not intended for you:
let it divide itself touching your cheeks
to join again, tremblingly, behind you.

O blessed beings, o you who are whole,
you who appear as the heart's beginning.
Bows for the arrows, and target of arrows,
eternally shines your tear-stained smile.

Be not afraid to suffer: let all that is
heavy return to the weight of the earth.
Heavy are mountains, and heavy the seas.

Even those trees you planted as children
long since grew heavy beyond all your strength.
Oh, for the breezes...... oh, for the spaces.....

SONNETS TO ORPHEUS

(Book I, #5)

*E*rect no stone to his memory. Instead
let the rose bloom every year to honor him.
For the rose *is* Orpheus! He appears in
various guises in his metamorphosis.

Do not trouble to find other names for him:
it is always Orpheus when you hear singing.
He comes and goes. Is it not much like a gift
when he outlasts some days the bowl of roses?

Oh, he must leave; it is for you to grasp this,
as much as he is frightened by his leaving.
But while his word surpasses his being here,

he is already there where none can follow.
The lyre's strings no longer ensnare his hands.
And he obeys as he enters the beyond.

SONNETS TO ORPHEUS

(Book I, #9)

*O*nly who holds the lyre
among the shadows
may be allowed to render
the infinite praise.

Only who with the dead shared
their own poppy seeds
will never lose the sound of
their softest of tones.

The reflection at times may
seem blurred in the pool:
know the image.

**Only in the two-fold realm
do voices become
eternal and mild.**

SONNETS TO ORPHEUS

(Book I, #10)

*Y*ou, who have never left my memory,
I greet you, ancient sarcophagi,
through which the happy song of the waters
flows ever changing as in Roman days;

or those that lie open, resembling the
joyful eyes of an awakening shepherd,—
stillness within, safe for an errant bee
and escaping fluttering butterflies—:

all of you who have been freed from doubt,
I greet you, whose mouths once more are open,
who have long known what deepest silence is.

Do we know, friends, what is and what is not?
Both questions form the hesitant hour
reflected in the human countenance.

SONNETS TO ORPHEUS

(Book I, #12)

*W*elcome, o spirit that may unite us;
for we live our lives in changing ways,
and with little steps our clocks keep pacing
as they measure our essential days.

Without really knowing our true place
we act out of actual concern.
Our antennas reach out to antennas,
and the empty far-off distance proved

pure tension. O music of the forces!
Is not every interruption with you
caused by our daily working lives?

Even though the farmer works and worries
as the seed is transformed into summer:
it is not enough. The earth *bestows*.

SONNETS TO ORPHEUS

(Book I, #13)

*F*ull ripened apple, pear and banana,
gooseberry too... All of these fruits bespeak
of life and death into the mouth... I sense...
Read it upon the face of any child

how it reacts to taste. This comes from afar.
Does something slowly change within your mouth?
Where otherwise were words, now liquids flow
freed from the fruit which stored it in its flesh.

Put into words what Apple means to you.
This sweetness, when it starts to concentrate
and on your palate delicately raised

turns clear, awake, becomes transparent, takes
on a double meaning, sunny, earthy, here ---:
Experience, O Sense of Joy --, immense!

SONNETS TO ORPHEUS

(Book I, #19)

*T*hough the world changes its image
as sudden as clouds change their forms,
all things that have reached perfection
return to their primeval source.

Above the changing and roaming,
farther and freer,
is still heard your earliest song,
god with the lyre.

Unrecognized go our pains,
nor have we ever learned to love,
and what in death separates us

is never unveiled.
Only your song over the land
hallows and extols.

SONNETS TO ORPHEUS

(Book II, #4)

O this is the animal that never lived.
Though people did not know this, yet they were
filled with love for this shy creature -- its gentle
gait and bearing, the slender neck and quiet look.

Although it never *was,* yet through the people's
love the perfect creature happened. They always
provided space, an open clearing, to roam,
to lift its head with ease, and hardly needed

to be! They never nourished it with grain,
but gave the feeling that this would be done, if
ever needed. This gave the animal such

strength: it grew a horn out of its brow. One horn.
To a virgin it advanced -- all white and chaste --
and was in the silver-mirror and in her.

SONNETS TO ORPHEUS

(Book II, #6)

O rose, enthroned flower, for men in ancient times
you were a chalice fashioned with a simple rim.
But for *us,* now, you are the countless flowering rose,
the object of our inexhaustible delight.

Within your riches you reveal raiment upon
raiment that clothe a body that is dazzling light.
But a single petal of your blossom renders
comparison with any raiment obsolete.

Throughout the centuries your fragrance has evoked
the sweetest names, wafting across the seas to us;
and suddenly the air is laden with your scent.

Elusive. We cannot really name it, but guess . . .
while memories meet it across the centuries
that we have summoned: hours from the distant past.

SONNETS TO ORPHEUS

(Book II, #15)

*O*fountain-head, whose never silent mouth
speaks endlessly of all that's great and pure, --
you, whose marble mask is reflected in
the flowing waters that the viaduct

carries from distant wells. From the steep slopes
of the high Appenines, past ancient graves,
they bring to you their messages, as they
run down your weathered blackened chin into

the waiting basin. This is the sleeping
reclining ear, the marble ear, into
which you whisper tales of their long journey.

Ear of the earth. Only with itself the
fountain speaks. If someone moves a jug between
you, it thinks you caused the interruption.

SONNETS TO ORPHEUS

(Book II, #29)

*S*ilent friend of far-off distances, feel
how still your breath enhances our space.
Let the bells high in the darkened belfry
ring out for you! That which weakens you

will turn to strength upon this nourishment.
Transformed, you may freely come and go.
What experience has made you suffer most?
If to drink tastes bitter, become wine!

Let the magic powers of this night's
excess, at the crossroads of your senses,
give meaning to this strange encounter.

When the world has long forgotten you,
to the silent earth say: I am flowing.
To the rushing waters speak: I am!

DUINO ELEGIES

(DIE DUINESER ELEGIEN)

(1912–1922)

The property of Princess
Marie von Thurn und Taxis-Hohenlohe

THE FIRST ELEGY

*W*ho, if I cried out, would hear me among the angels'
hierarchies? and even if one of them suddenly
pressed me against his heart, I would perish
in the embrace of his stronger existence.
For beauty is nothing but the beginning of terror
which we are barely able to endure and are awed
because it serenely disdains to annihilate us.
Each single angel is terrifying.
And so I force myself, swallow and hold back
the surging call of my dark sobbing.
Oh, to whom can we turn for help?
Not angels, not humans;
and even the knowing animals are aware that we feel
little secure and at home in our interpreted world.
There remains perhaps some tree on a hillside
daily for us to see; yesterday's street remains for us,
and the loyalty of a habit so much at ease with us
stayed, moved in with us and showed no signs of leaving.
Oh, and the night, the night, when the wind

full of cosmic space invades our frightened faces.
Whom would it not remain for—that longed-after,
gently disenchanting night, painfully there for the
solitary heart to achieve? Is it easier for lovers?
Don't you know *yet?* Fling out of your arms the emptiness
into the spaces we breathe—perhaps the birds will feel
the expanded air in their more fervent flight.

Yes, the springtimes were in need of you. Often a star
waited for you to espy it and sense its light.
A wave rolled toward you out of the distant past,
or as you walked below an open window,
a violin gave itself to your hearing.
All this was trust. But could you manage it?
Were you not always distraught by expectation,
as if all this were announcing the arrival
of a beloved? (Where would you find a place
to hide her, with all your great strange thoughts
coming and going and often staying for the night.)
When longing overcomes you, sing of women in love;
for their famous passion is far from immortal enough.
Those whom you almost envy, the abandoned and
desolate ones, whom you found so much more loving
than those gratified. Begin ever new again
the praise you cannot attain; remember:
the hero lives on and survives; even his downfall
was for him only a pretext for achieving
his final birth. But nature, exhausted, takes lovers
back into itself, as if such creative forces could never be

achieved a second time.
Have you thought of Gaspara Stampa[1] sufficiently:

that any girl abandoned by her lover may feel
from that far intenser example of loving:
"Ah, might I become like her!" Should not their oldest
sufferings finally become more fruitful for us?
Is it not time that lovingly we freed ourselves
from the beloved and, quivering, endured:
as the arrow endures the bow-string's tension,
and in this tense release becomes more than itself.
For staying is nowhere.

Voices, voices. Listen my heart, as only saints
have listened: until the gigantic call lifted them
clear off the ground. Yet they went on, impossibly,
kneeling, completely unawares: *so* intense was
their listening. Not that you could endure
the voice of God—far from it! But listen
to the voice of the wind and the ceaseless message
that forms itself out of silence. They sweep
toward you now from those who died young.
Whenever you entered a church in Rome or Naples,
did not their fate quietly speak to you as recently
as the tablet did in Santa Maria Formosa?[2]
What do they want of me? to quietly remove
the appearance of suffered injustice that,
at times, hinders a little their spirits from
freely proceeding onward.

Of course, it is strange to inhabit the earth no longer,
to no longer use skills one had barely time to acquire;
not to observe roses and other things that promised
so much in terms of a human future, no longer
to be what one was in infinitely anxious hands;
to even discard one's own name as easily as a child
abandons a broken toy.
Strange, not to desire to continue wishing one's wishes.
Strange to notice all that was related, fluttering
so loosely in space. And being dead is hard work
and full of retrieving before one can gradually feel a
trace of eternity.—Yes, but the living make
the mistake of drawing too sharp a distinction.
Angels (they say) are often unable to distinguish
between moving among the living or the dead.
The eternal torrent whirls all ages along with it,
through both realms forever, and their voices are lost in
its thunderous roar.

In the end the early departed have no longer
need of us. One is gently weaned from things
of this world as a child outgrows the need
of its mother's breast. But we who have need
of those great mysteries, we for whom grief is
so often the source of spiritual growth,
could we exist without them?
Is the legend vain that tells of music's beginning

in the midst of the mourning for Linos?[3]
the daring first sounds of song piercing
the barren numbness, and how in that stunned space
an almost godlike youth suddenly left forever,
and the emptiness felt for the first time
those harmonious vibrations which now enrapture
and comfort and help us.

THE FOURTH ELEGY

O trees of life, oh, what when winter comes?
We are not of one mind. Are not like birds
in unison migrating. And overtaken,
overdue, we thrust ourselves into the wind
and fall to earth into indifferent ponds.
Blossoming and withering we comprehend as one.
And somewhere lions roam, quite unaware,
in their magnificence, of any weakness.

But we, while wholly concentrating on one thing,
already feel the pressure of another.
Hatred is our first response. And lovers,
are they not forever invading one another's
bounderies?—although they promised space,
hunting and homeland. Then, for a sketch
drawn at a moment's impulse, a ground of contrast
is prepared, painfully, so that we may see.
For they are most exact with us. We do not know
the contours of our feelings. We only know
what shapes them from outside.

Who has not sat, afraid, before his own heart's
curtain? It lifted and displayed the scenery
of departure. Easy to understand. The well-known
garden swaying just a little. Then came the dancer.
Not *he!* Enough! However lightly he pretends to move:
he is just disguised, costumed, an ordinary man
who enters through the kitchen when coming home.
I will not have these half-filled human masks;
better the puppet. It at least is full.
I will endure this well-stuffed doll, the wire,
the face that is nothing but appearance. Here out front
I wait. Even if the lights go down and I am told:
"There's nothing more to come,"—even if
the grayish drafts of emptiness come drifting down
from the deserted stage—even if not one
of my now silent forebears sits beside me
any longer, not a woman, not even a boy—[4]
he with the brown and squinting eyes—:
I'll still remain. For one can always watch.

Am I not right? You, to whom life would taste[5]
so bitter, Father, after you—for my sake—
sipped of mine, that first muddy infusion
of my necessity. You kept on tasting, Father,
as I kept on growing, troubled by the aftertaste
of my so strange a future as you kept searching
my unfocused gaze—you who, so often since

you died, have been afraid for my well-being,
within my deepest hope, relinquishing that calmness,
the realms of equanimity such as the dead possess
for my so small a fate— Am I not right?

And you, my parents, am I not right? You who loved me
for that small beginning of my love for you
from which I always shyly turned away, because
the distance in your features grew, changed,
even while I loved it, into cosmic space
where you no longer were. . . . . : and when I feel
inclined to wait before the puppet stage, no,
rather to stare at it so intensely that in the end
to counter-balance my searching gaze, an angel
has to come on as an actor, and begin manipulating
the lifeless bodies of the puppets to perform.
Angel and puppet! Now at last there is a play!
Then what we separate can come together by our
very presence. And only then the entire cycle
of our own life-seasons is revealed and set in motion.
Above, beyond us, the angel plays. Look:
must not the dying notice how unreal, how full
of pretense is all that we accomplish here, where
nothing is to be itself. O hours of childhood,
when behind each shape more than the past lay hidden,
when that which lay before us was not the future.

We grew, of course, and sometimes were impatient
in growing up, half for the sake of pleasing those
with nothing left but their own grown-upness.
Yet, when alone, we entertained ourselves
with what alone endures, we would stand there
in the infinite space that spans the world and toys,
upon a place, which from the first beginning
had been prepared to serve a pure event.

Who shows a child just as it stands? Who places him
within his constellation, with the measuring-rod
of distance in his hand. Who makes his death
from gray bread that grows hard,—or leaves
it there inside his rounded mouth, jagged as the core
of a sweet apple? . . . . . . The minds of murderers
are easily comprehended. But this: to contain death,
the whole of death, even *before* life has begun,
to hold it all so gently within oneself,
and not be angry: that is indescribable.

THE FIFTH ELEGY

(inspired by Picasso's painting: "The Family of the
Saltimbanques") dedicated to Frau Hertha Koenig

*W*hoever *are* they, tell me, these wayfaring troupers,
even more transient than we ourselves,—so urgently,
from earliest childhood, obsessed by a never-satisfied *Will*—
to please *whom*? Yet it continues to wring them, bend them,
toss them, twist them, catch them and toss them again:—
as through an oil-slippery air they descend and land
on the threadbare carpet, worn thin by their endless leaping
and tumbling, this carpet lost in space. Laid on like a plaster,
as though the suburban sky had injured the earth.

                                            And barely there,
erect, in place and to be seen—the alphabet's capital D ...
encircling the assembled acrobats as if in jest: Daring ...
yet even the strongest men are rolled once more, playful,
by that forever ready grip, rolled like the pewter plate
that Augustus the Strong crushed and twisted at table.[7]

Ah, and around this center
the Rose of Onlooking:

blooming and shedding its petals.
Around this pestle, the pistil, pregnant with its own
flowering pollen, re-fertilized to bear the false fruit
of disgust they are never conscious of,—
gleaming like the thinnest veneer
of a sham-smiling surface.
There: the withered, wrinkled weight-lifter,
the old man, who now can only beat the drum,
shrunk within his powerful skin that now looks
as if once it held *two* men, while the one already
lay in the churchyard and the other survives him,
deaf and sometimes a little confused, in the widowed skin.
But the young one, the man, as if he were
the son of a neck and a nun: taut and powerfully filled
with muscles and innocence.

Oh, you,
whom a grief that was still quite small,
once received as a plaything, during one
of its long convalescences. . . .

You, who with a thud only known to unripe fruit
fall daily a hundred times from the tree
of mutually constructed emotions,
(which, swifter than water, in minutes, rushes
through spring, summer and autumn)—
falling and rebounding on the grave[8]:

sometimes, during a half-pause, you feel
a look of love surging across your face
turned toward your seldom affectionate mother;
yet it loses itself on your body, whose surface
quickly absorbs it, that shy and barely attempted face. . . .
And again the man claps his hands for your leap,
and before you are aware of a pain
near your ever galloping heart, the burning
in the soles of your feet rushes ahead of that earlier pain,
chasing a few bodily tears quickly into your eyes.
And, nevertheless, blindly,
the smile. . . .

Angel! O take it, gather that small-flowering herb
of healing. Create a vase, preserve it!
Set it among those joys not *yet* open to us;
in a lovely urn praise it with a soaring
florid inscription:
                                    "Subrisio Saltat."[9]

You then, lovely one,
you whom the most exquisite joys
have silently passed over.
Perhaps the fringes of your shawl are happy for you—
or perhaps the green metallic silk
taut across your firm young breasts,
feels itself endlessly spoiled, missing nothing.
You,

display fruit of equanimity,
set out before the public, forever changing,
on all the wavering scales of balance,
openly below your shoulders.

Where, o *where* is the place—I carry it in my heart—
where they were still far from being *able,*
where they still fell away from each other
like mounting animals not yet properly paired:—
where the weights are still heavy,
where from their vainly twirling rods
the plates still wobble and drop. . . .

And suddenly in this wearisome Nowhere, suddenly
the unspeakable place, where pure inadequacy
incomprehensibly changes—, leaps over into that
empty 'too-much'; where the many-digited sum
solves into naught.

Squares, o square in Paris, infinite show-place,
where Madame Lamort the milliner twists and winds
the restless paths of the world, those endless ribbons,
fashioning from them ever-new creations of bows,
frills, flowers, cockades and artificial fruits,—
all dyed in sham colors,—to decorate the cheap
winter bonnets of Fate.

Angel: granted there were a place
of which we did not know,
and there, upon an unspeakable carpet,
lovers could show all that here they are forever
unable to master—their daring lofty leaps of heartflight,
their towers of passion, their ladders long since
propped against each other where there was no ground,
trembling,—and were able to master it, before the circle
of spectators, the countless silent dead:
Would these, then, throw down their last, forever
saved-up, forever hidden, which we do not know,
eternally valid coins of happiness before the at last
truly smiling pair upon that stilled carpet?

THE SIXTH ELEGY

igtree, how long ago have I discovered meaning
in your unchanging disregard for blossoming,
while into the seasonably determined fruit, unproclaimed,
you urge your purest secret.
Like a fountain's curved pipe, your arching boughs
force the sap downward and up, and it leaps from sleep.
hardly awake, into the joy of its sweetest achievement.
Look: the God in the swan.
                       . . . But we still linger, sadly,
for we glory in flowering; already betrayed
we reach the retarded core of our ultimate fruit.
In only a few does the urge for action mount strongly
that they already stand, aglow in their heart's fullness,
when the temptation to bloom touches their youthful lips,
touches their eyelids like the soothing night air:
Heroes, perhaps, and like those destined to die young,
in whom Death the gardener has otherwise twisted their veins.
These go plunging onward, ahead of their victorious smile,
like the span of noble stallions before the conquering King
as seen on the gently molded bas-reliefs at Karnak.[10]

How wondrously near is the hero to those early departed.
Permanence does not concern him. His rising is in *Being.*
Steadfastly he takes himself and enters the changed constellatic
of his perpetual danger. Few could find him there.
But Fate that darkly conceals us, suddenly inspired,
sings him into the storm of her turbulent world.
I hear no one like *him.* All at once I am pierced
by his darkling voice, carried on the streaming air.

Then, how gladly would I hide myself from this longing:
Oh, were I, were I a boy and could still become one,
and sit, propped up upon my growing arms, reading of Samson,
how his mother at first bore nothing, and afterward all.

Was he not hero already, within you, o mother,
and did not his imperious choosing begin there, within you?
Thousands teemed inside your womb and wished to be *him.*
But look: he seized and refused, chose and prevailed.
And if he demolished pillars, it was when he burst forth
from the world of your body out into the narrower world,
where he continued choosing and prevailing.
O mothers of heroes! Sources of ravaging rivers!
You gorges, down into which virgins have plunged,

weeping, high from the rim of the heart,—
sacrifices to the son. For whenever the hero stormed
through the stays of love, each heartbeat intended for him
could only lift him beyond it; turning away, he stood,
at the end of the smiles,—transfigured.

THE TENTH ELEGY

*T*hat some day, emerging at last from the terrifying vision
I may burst into jubilant praise to assenting angels!
That of the clear-struck keys of the heart not one may fail
to sound because of a loose, doubtful or broken string!
That my streaming countenance may make me more resplende
That my humble weeping change into blossoms.
Oh, how will you then, nights of suffering, be remembered
with love. Why did I not kneel more fervently, disconsolate
sisters, more bendingly kneel to receive you, more loosely
surrender myself to your loosened hair? We, squanderers of pai
gazing beyond them to judge the end of their duration.
They are only our winter's foliage, our somber evergreen,
one of the seasons of our interior year,—not only season,
but place, settlement, camp, soil and dwelling.

How woeful, strange, are the alleys of the City of Pain,
where in the false silence created from too much noise,
a thing cast out from the mold of emptiness
swaggers that gilded hubbub, the bursting memorial.
Oh, how completely an angel would stamp out their market
of solace, bounded by the church, bought ready for use:

as clean, disappointing and closed as a post office on Sunday.
Farther out, though, there are always the rippling edges
of the fair. Seasaws of freedom! High-divers and jugglers of zeal!
And the shooting-gallery's targets of bedizened happiness:
targets tumbling in tinny contortions whenever some better
marksman happens to hit one. From cheers to chance he goes
staggering on, as booths that can please the most curious tastes
are drumming and bawling. For adults only there is something
special to see: how money multiplies. Anatomy made amusing!
Money's organs on view! Nothing concealed! Instructive,
and guaranteed to increase fertility! . . .

          Oh, and then outside,
behind the farthest billboard, pasted with posters for 'Deathless',
that bitter beer tasting quite sweet to drinkers,
if they chew fresh diversions with it. . . .
Behind the billboard, just in back of it, life is real.
Children play, and lovers hold each other,—aside,
earnestly, in the trampled grass, and dogs respond to nature.
The youth continues onward; perhaps he is in love with
a young Lament. . . . he follows her into the meadows.
She says: the way is long. We live out there. . . .

          Where? And the youth
follows. He is touched by her gentle bearing. The shoulders,
the neck,—perhaps she is of noble ancestry?
Yet he leaves her, turns around, looks back and waves. . . .
What could come of it? She is a Lament.

Only those who died young, in their first state of
timeless serenity, while they are being weaned,

follow her lovingly. She waits for girls
and befriends them. Gently she shows them
what she is wearing. Pearls of grief
and the fine-spun veils of patience.—
With youths she walks in silence.

But there, where they live, in the valley,
an elderly Lament responds to the youth as he asks:—
We were once, she says, a great race, we Laments.
Our fathers worked the mines up there in the mountains;
sometimes among men you will find a piece of polished
primeval pain, or a petrified slag from an ancient volcano.
Yes, that came from there. Once we were rich.—

And she leads him gently through the vast landscape
of Lamentation, shows him the columns of temples,
the ruins of strongholds from which long ago
the princes of Lament wisely governed the country.
Shows him the tall trees of tears,
the fields of flowering sadness,
(the living know them only as softest foliage);
shows him the beasts of mourning, grazing—
and sometimes a startled bird, flying straight through
their field of vision, far away traces the image of its
solitary cry.—
At evening she leads him to the graves of elders
of the race of Lamentation, the sybils and prophets.
With night approaching, they move more softly,
and soon there looms ahead, bathed in moonlight,

the sepulcher, that all-guarding ancient stone.
Twin-brother to that on the Nile, the lofty Sphinx—:
the silent chamber's countenance.
They marvel at the regal head that has, forever silent,
laid the features of mankind upon the scales of the stars.

His sight, still blinded by his early death,
cannot grasp it. But the Sphinx's gaze
frightens an owl from the rim of the double-crown.[11]
The bird, with slow down-strokes, brushes
along the cheek, that with the roundest curve,
and faintly inscribes on the new death-born hearing,
as though on the double page of an opened book,
the indescribable outline.

And higher up, the stars. New ones. Stars
of the land of pain. Slowly she names them:
"There, look: the *Rider,* the *Staff,* and that crowded
constellation they call the *Garland of Fruit.*
Then farther up toward the Pole:
Cradle, Way, the *Burning Book, Doll, Window.*
And in the Southern sky, pure as the lines
on the palm of a blessed hand, the clear sparkling M,
standing for Mothers. . . ."

Yet the dead youth must go on alone.
In silence the elder Lament brings him
as far as the gorge where it shimmers in the moonlight:

The Fountainhead of Joy. With reverence she names it,
saying: "In the world of mankind it is a life-bearing stream."

They reach the foothills of the mountain,
and there she embraces him, weeping.

Alone, he climbs the mountains of primeval pain.
Not even his footsteps ring from this soundless fate.

But were these timeless dead to awaken an image for us,
see, they might be pointing to the catkins, hanging
from the leafless hazels, or else they might mean
the rain that falls upon the dark earth in early Spring.

And we, who always think
of happiness as *rising* feel the emotion
that almost overwhelms us
whenever a happy thing *falls*.

EXPLANATORY NOTES TO THE ELEGIES

FIRST ELEGY

1 Gaspara Stampa. Italian poetess born 1523 in Padua. At age 26 she fell in love with a young Venetian nobleman. The joys and sorrows of her love are recorded in over two hundred sonnets. She died in 1554 at the age of 31.

2 Santa Maria Formosa. When Rilke speaks of the "early departed", and "those who died young", he recalls a marble plaque discovered near the altar of this medieval church in Venice which bears the inscription (in Latin):
"While life was granted me, I lived for others. Now, after death, I have not perished, but in cold marble I live for myself. I was Hermann Wilhelm. Flanders mourns for me, Adria sighs for me, Poverty calls for me." The tablet bears the date of his death: October 16, 1593.

3. Linos—precursor of Orpheus in Greek mythology.

FOURTH ELEGY

4 The lines: . . . *"not a woman, not even a boy—he with the brown and squinting eyes . . ."* refers to his cousin, Egon von Rilke, who died in childhood. Rilke wrote of him: "I often think of him and keep returning to that figure which has remained for me indescribably affecting. Much of childhood, the sadness and helplessness of childhood, is embodied for me in his form . . . in his beautiful brown eyes, disfigured by a squint."

5 To understand the father-son relationship which Rilke describes in this Elegy, one must know of the unfulfilled love between them. Rilke was ten years

old when his parents separated. His father died while Rilke was still an adolescent. Of his father he wrote: "When I think back, how I—in the face of the utmost difficulties trying to understand and come to terms with each other—how I loved my father! Often, in childhood, my thoughts became confused, bewildered, and my heart froze at the very thought that one day he may no longer be."

FIFTH ELEGY

6 This elegy was inspired by Picasso's famous painting *The Family of the Saltimbanques,* now in the permanent collection of the National Gallery, Washington. Rilke knew and admired Picasso in Paris. He also knew Frau Hertha Koenig of Munich, who acquired the painting. When Rilke returned to Munich he had difficulties finding suitable quarters. Learning of Frau Koenig's plans to spend the summer and fall at her estate in Westphalia, he asked whether he could view the painting during her absence. She then invited him to move into her house where he stayed from June until October. The result was this the last written of the Duino Elegies which he gratefully dedicated to Frau Koenig. In a letter to a friend he wrote: "I am studying this loveliest of Picasso's paintings, in which there is so much of Paris that, at times, I forget that I am not there."

7 Augustus the Strong. Rilke refers here to August II, King of Poland (1670–1733). Called "The Strong" because of his prodigious strength, notorious drinking bouts and sexual prowess. It was said that he fathered over one hundred children!

8 The Stanzas: *"You, who with a thud known to un-ripe fruit / fall daily a hundred times from the tree / of mutually constructed emotions. . . . / falling and rebounding on the grave . . ."* refers to the human tree, or pyramid, formed daily by the acrobats.

9 *"Subrisio Saltat"* is an abbreviation for *subrisio sal-tatoris*—the acrobat's smile.

SIXTH ELEGY

10 Karnak, Egypt. It was at the great temple of Amon-Ra at Karnak, located in the Valley of the Kings, that Rilke observed the delicately moulded reliefs of the team of magnificent horses that draw the chariot of the conquering King.

TENTH ELEGY

11 The Sphinx, Egypt. In his description of the Sphinx's double-crown Rilke uses the Arabic *pschent*—the emblem worn by the rulers of Egypt's two Kingdoms: the Upper and Lower Nile.

A. E. F.

COLLECTED POEMS

FROM THE YEARS 1906 TO 1926

(GESAMMELTE GEDICHTE

AUS DEN JAHREN 1906 BIS 1926)

ALMOND TREES IN BLOOM

(Ronda near Malaga, Spain.)

*U*nendingly I marvel at your flowering,
the wonder of your existence, o blessed trees,
as you continue, forever renewing, to
bear these so soon to vanish exquisite blossoms.

Oh, he who unlocks the secret of flowering:
his heart will rise above the smallest of dangers
and will meet the greatest of them, death, without fear.

SPANISH TRILOGY

(Ronda, Spain.)

(Part I)

$\mathcal{O}$ut of this cloud, see: that hides the star so wildly
with its shadow, which just now was -- (and me),
out of the mountain range, now darkened by the night
with night-winds blowing for some time -- (and me),
out of the valley's river, catching reflections
of the cloud-torn light of heaven -- (and me):
out of me and all these things to fashion
a single unit, Lord: out of me, and the feeling
that the herd shares inside the safety of the shed,
as they, exhaling, accept the great dark no-longer-being
of the world outside: --- of me and every light
shining in the darkness of the many houses, Lord:
to create *one unit:* out of the strangers
of whom I know not one, Lord, and me and me
to fashion *one thing:* out of those sleeping --
strange old men in hospital beds who cough
as if it were important, and out of children
resting drowsy with sleep against strange breasts;
out of the many unidentifiable things,
and always me, out of nothing but me and those
whom I do not know, to create *that thing:*

Lord, Lord, Lord, that thing,
that world-like earthen like a meteor in its heaviness
only manages the total sum of flight:
bringing nothing with it but its own weight.

(Part II)

W hy must someone go and take upon himself
strange things, as one who carries a market basket,
which he keeps filling more and more as he passes
from stand to stand, and leaving cannot say:
Lord, wherefore this feast?

Why must someone stand like a shepherd, so exposed
to the overflowing measure of receiving,
so involved in taking part in what is going on,
that he would rather lean against a tree out in the country
and contemplate his destiny without further action.
He does not have in his far-reaching sight
the quiet relaxation of his flock. He has
nothing but world, world in every glance, and world
in every inclination. Things trouble him
that others welcome, things uninvited, like music
that enters blindly into the blood and changes
as it passes on.

It is then that he rises in the night, awakened
by the bird's first call, and once outside feels
his whole being filled with courage, as he, upon his face,
feels the shining magnitude of all the stars, heavy ---
oh, not like one, who has prepared this night for his beloved,
to pamper her with all the tendernesses
of the heavens.

(Part III)

*T*hat I may always - when I am once again
surrounded by the cities' jostling crowds,
the deafening noise and chaos of traffic -
separately - amidst this dense commotion, -
remember heaven and the mountain range
from where the herds would now be homeward bound.
Stone-like be my courage, and the shepherd's
daily routine seems possible for me,
as he goes about, tanned, and with measured skill
tosses the stone accurately with his crook
to keep his flock from straying beyond his chosen border.
With measured steps, not lightly, with body bent
and wrapped in thought ---

But when he stands in silence, he is magnificent.
Even now a god could secretly disguise himself
as such a shepherd without losing his godliness.
Alternatingly he stays and goes, as does each day,
and shadows of the clouds pass over him
as if space itself were thinking leisurely thoughts for him.

Be it whatever he may mean to you.
Like the wavering flame of the night-light's candle
I place myself within the lamp's protective cylinder.
The shining then becomes steady. But death
would find it easier to attain.

TO THE ANGEL

(Ronda, Spain, 1913)

O strong and silent angel, placed high
above the night, how strong your beacon shines
and penetrates our earthly darkness, through
which in vain we try to find our way.

Ours is: unable to discover
the exit leading out of our lives'
inner confusion, which your light outlines
like the sun's last rays the mountains peaks.

Your delights are far above our world
and we can never comprehend your deeds:
like the purest night of spring's equinox
you stand, separating day from day.

Who would ever venture to confess
to you the mixtures that our lives afflict?
You enjoy the glories of all greatness,
while our lives of little things consist.

When we weep, we seem only to be moved,
and when we look, we are at best awake;
our smiles reveal little of seduction,
and if they did, would anyone follow us?

Angel, is it I who cries and cries?
Yet how could this lamentation be mine?
Oh, I shout and beat my wooden clappers
and have the feeling no one ever hears.

And my crying is of no avail
if you do not touch me, because I *am*.
Shine, oh keep on shining! Make me known
to the distant stars. For I am fading.....

IN THE BEGINNING...

(Paris, January 1914)

*E*ver since those wondrous days of the Creation
our Lord God sleeps: we are His sleep.
And He accepted this in His indulgence,
resigned to rest among the distant stars.

Our actions stopped Him from reacting,
for His fist-tight hand is numbed by sleep,
and the times brought in the age of heroes
during which our dark hearts plundered Him.

Sometimes He appears as if tormented,
and His body jerks as if plagued by pain;
but these spells are always outweighed by the
number of His countless other worlds.

SUFFERING

(Paris, Autumn 1913)

*I*s suffering not good - as when the ploughshare is
ready and secured to break another furrow -
is suffering not beneficial? And who is
the last one who disrupts all our suffering?

How much there is to suffer. When was time enough
to pay attention to our lighter emotions?
And still I recognize, better than most others
who will be resurrected, what blessedness is.

REFLECTION

(Ronda, Spain, 1913)

*I*s there nothing more left for me next?
Shall I remain only a while longer?
(Often my weeping disturbs
and my smiling distorts),
but at times I recognize
in the light of the healing flame
intimately my innermost heart.

My heart, that once so tenderly
responded to the spring of life,
even though it was carefully
stored away in the cellars of life.
Oh, how it was at once prepared
daringly to undertake the greatest of ascents,
climbing and understanding like a star
the descending night.

ST. CHRISTOPHER AND THE CHRIST CHILD

*H*is towering strength, his giant frame and build
predestined him to serve the greatest Lord.
Before, he had companioned knights and kings.
For him they lacked the greatness that he sought.

He waited for the Saviour of Mankind
of whom the legend told: Leave all behind:
wife, chattel, home and child, and follow me!
Through me ye shall gain life, and wisdom, faith and truth.

He was a fordsman now. Wanting to serve.
He carried pilgrims traveling from afar
across the mighty stream by day and night
in answer to their calls, faint, from the other side.

With sturdy legs he challenged the water's treacherous course,
fording the river safely, avoiding its pitfalls.
Then, bending ever so gently after reaching shore
he would release unharmed his human charge once more.

Ancient one! Forebear of future bridges yet to come,
whose curving granite arches would leap the rivers' span.

His humble dwelling, close by the river's bend,
provided comfort. And, relaxed and breathing deeply,
he drove away the tiredness of the day
as slumber brought relief and welcome rest.

But even while he slept he was aware,
and in his dreams he listened for the calls.

Suddenly he woke! He sat up, listening,
startled by a voice so high in tone: a child's!
And rising from his bed he hurried out
searching the darkened shore for signs of life.

But knowing well how easily children flee from fright,
he dwarfed his powerful shape, crouched in the doorway low,
advanced with bended knees, and with a father's smile.
But found no child outside. The wild wind roamed the night.

He mumbled to himself, still listening for the sound,
and said: How could a child be there, out in the stormy night?
And turning back, retiring with one big stride to bed,
he soon was fast asleep.

Listen!
For there it was again, this pitiable plaintive call.
He took one look outside -- out there deep darkness reigned,
with only the wild wind whirling and sighing in the trees.

I'm sure there's no one there, or am I going blind?
Reproached himself for failing, and went to sleep once more.

But soon he woke again! This time there was no doubt!
For now the high-pitched voice was nearer than before,
pleading, imploring, begging.
It struck him to the core with overpowering force:

Lo, outside there stood a child!

THE DEATH OF MOSES

*N*ot one of the angels, only the dark fallen one,
was willing; armed with a deadly weapon he approached
the chosen one. But hardly advanced he fell crashing
backward, and upward to the heavens he shouted:
I cannot!

For, relaxed, looking up from under his bushy
eyebrows, Moses had been fully aware of him,
but had continued in his writing: Words of blessing,
of the eternally enduring name of God.
And his eyes remained clear to the depth of his strength.

Thereupon the Lord, tearing half of the heavens
with Him in His wake, swept down and opened up
by Himself the mountain and prepared a resting place
in which He laid the aged man. He then called the soul
out of its orderly habitation: Come, arise!
And the two had much in common to relate, recounting
endless tales of their timeless friendship.

But in the end the soul felt: it was enough.
That it had been enough the consecrated one agreed.
Then bent God the Father His countenance slowly
down to the aged Moses, took him with His kiss
out of him into His age, the infinitely older.
And with His hands, God the Creator buried him
within the mountain's safekeeping: so that there should be
only one, a newly created one, resting beneath
the mountains of the earth, unknown to man.

HEARTBEAT

(Muzot, November 1923)

*O*nly mouths are we. Who sings the distant heart
which safely exists in the center of all things?
His giant heartbeat is diverted in us
into little pulses. And his giant grief
is, like his giant jubilation, far too
great for us. And so we tear ourselves away
from him time after time, remaining only
mouths. But unexpectedly and secretly
the giant heartbeat enters our being,
so that we scream ------,
and are transformed in being and in countenance.

TO THE BELOVED

*B*eloved, we who seem destined never to meet:
I do not know what music you love best.
No longer do I try to find you, seek you
when fervent longing for you overwhelms me.

All the great images in me: remembered landscapes,
towns and towers, bridges and unexpected
turns of roads traversing vast imposing lands,
over which in ancient times the gods once wandered:

All these memories rise up again because of you.
You who are vanishing from me.....

Oh, you are the gardens I once envisioned,
the vistas that filled me with so much hope.
An open window in a country house ---
you almost came toward me, lost in thought.
Pathways I found upon which you had walked
just recently......

Sometimes in mirrored shop windows I see
your face reflected, startling me so that
I almost faint, only to find myself staring
at my own image.

Who knows whether the song of the same bird
did not reverberate within us both,
separately, last evening.

O TELL US, POET

O tell us, poet, what it is you do?
                                    -- I praise.
But in the midst of deadly turmoil, what
helps you endure, and how do you survive?
                                    -- I praise.
And that which nameless is, anonymous,
how do you, poet, still call out to them?
                                    -- I praise.
Who grants your right to pose in any guise,
wear any mask, and still remain sincere?
                                    -- I praise.
And that the stillness and the violence -
like star and storm - know and acknowledge you?

                            :-- because I praise.

FALLING STARS

(Muzot, June 1924)

$\mathcal{D}$o you remember still the falling stars
that like swift horses through the heavens raced
and suddenly leaped across the hurdles
of our wishes --- do you recall? And we
did make so many! For there were countless numbers
of stars: each time we looked above we were
astounded by the swiftness of their daring play,
while in our hearts we felt safe and secure
watching these brilliant bodies disintegrate,
knowing somehow we had survived their fall.

TO MUSIC

*M*usic: breath of statues. Perhaps:
silence of images. You: speech,
where all speech ends. You: time,
standing vertically parallel to our
vanishing hearts.

Feelings for whom? Oh, you transformer
of feelings into what? --: audible landscapes!
You stranger: Music. You who have outgrown
our heart's innermost space, and overpowering,
surge away from us.....in holy farewell:
where our deepest center surrounds us
as the most distant horizon,
as the other side of air:
pure,ˋ
immense,
no longer habitable.

SONG

(From the diaries of Malte Laurids Brigge)

*Y*ou, whom I do not tell that all night long
I lie weeping,
whose very being makes me feel wanting
like a cradle.

You, who do not tell me, that you lie awake
thinking of me: --
what, if we carried all these longings within us
without ever being overwhelmed by them,
letting them pass?
- - - - - - - - - - -
Look at these lovers, tormented by love,
when first they begin confessing,
how soon they lie!
- - - - - - - - - - -
You make me feel alone. I try imagining:
one moment it is you, then it's the soaring wind;
a fragrance comes and goes but never lasts.
Oh, within my arms I lost all whom I loved!
Only you remain, always reborn again.
For since I never held you, I hold you fast.

THE LOVERS

*S*ee how they grow as one in each other's arms!
How in their veins all becomes ardent desire.
Their bodies move like a rotating axis
round which their entangled beings circle.

Thirsting, they are offered a libation;
wake and watch: and they revive to see.
Oh, let them in themselves become submerged
so that they may survive each other's love.

ALWAYS AGAIN....

*A*lways again, even though we know the landscape of love,
and the little churchyard with its sorrowful names,
and the terrifying silence of the gorge
down which all others found their ending:

Always again, we two find ourselves wandering
under the ancient trees,
and as always, again we stretch ourselves out
amidst the flowers, and contemplate the heavens.

FORCE OF GRAVITY

(Muzot, Autumn 1924)

*C*enter of all gravity, you who draw your strength
from every direction; even when airborne
you regain your centre, your source of strength.

Standing upright: like a draught quenching one's thirst,
the force of gravity plunges it downward.

But out of someone asleep falls gently,
like out of a cloud bank laden with moisture,
the heaviness that is rich with rain.

EARLY SPRING

(Muzot, February 1924)

*H*arshness vanished. A sudden softness
has replaced the meadows' wintry grey.
Little rivulets of water changed
their singing accents. Tendernesses,

hesitantly, reach toward the earth
from space, and country lanes are showing
these unexpected subtle risings
that find expression in the empty trees.

SPRING

(Muzot, March 1924)

*O*nce more the sap begins to rise from darkness
where roots found nourishment deep in the earth;
returning back to light it climbs with greenness
hidden inside the trunk's protective bark.

The inner force of nature is renewing
itself, preparing for the joys of spring;
a whole year's growth is rising up, unhindered,
into the barren branches of the crown.

The ancient chestnut tree stands ready, waiting
for yet another spring, though grey and cold,
while slender saplings tremble with excitement
at the arrival of the first young birds.

AUTUMN

(Muzot, Autumn 1924)

O tall upreaching tree, shedding your leaves:
now it demands of you to be ready
for the immensity of open sky
breaking through your barren branches.

Laden with the summer's richness, you seemed
deep and dense with shadows, appearing to us
almost like a lofty and confiding head.
But now your branches are like many roads
that outline the heavens. And the heavens know us not.

A last resort: we can pretend like birds in flight
passing through this newly created openness,
but are denied the right to use this space
that only deals with worlds. Our senses
search like waves upon the shore for closeness
and have to be content to flutter like a flag
unfurled, placed in the open sky ---

But our hearts still ache for your lovely head's lost crown.

NIGHT

(Muzot, October 1924)

*N*ight. O you whose countenance, dissolved
in deepness, hovers above my face.
You who are the heaviest counterweight
to my astounding contemplation.

Night, that trembles as reflected in my eyes,
but in itself is strong;
inexhaustible creation, dominant,
enduring beyond the earth's endurance;

Night, full of newly created stars that leave
trails of fire streaming from their seams
as they soar in inaudible adventure
through interstellar space:

how, overshadowed by your all-embracing vastness,
I appear minute! ----
Yet, being one with the ever more darkening earth,
I dare to be in you.

EXPOSED UPON THE MOUNTAINS OF THE HEART

*E*xposed upon the mountains of the heart.
Look how little there!
See: how small there lies the last domain of words,
and higher still and smaller yet the final
granary of feeling. Do you recognize it?

Left exposed upon the mountains of the heart.
Barren rock under your hands.
Yet there still blooms something here:
from out of the cleft rock an unknown flower
blossoms singing! But the knowing one? Oh, he began
to comprehend, is silent now, exposed
upon the mountains of the heart.

Here is, where full of confidence,
surefooted animals come roaming, stay awhile,
grazing, change directions, come and go.
And the giant bird of prey comes circling
around the mountain peak's pure refusal. --
But no longer finding shelter,
here upon the mountains of the heart....

FRUIT

(Muzot, January 1924)

*T*he sap rose up out of the earth, and climbed
and climbed, and was all secrecy inside
the fruit tree's sturdy trunk, till it reached up
into the swelling buds and became one
with the flaming blossoms of the flowers,
and then resumed its earlier silent task

throughout the summer's length, by day, by night,
bringing its fruitful sap up to the bearing tree
and knew itself as needed in its crowding
against the ever-expanding sympathetic space.

When now it is displayed in all its beauty,
ripeness and quiet wholesomeness, the oval
roundness rolls toward the fruit-bowl's middle
in which you placed it, as if scorning your
attention, and so returns to its own center.

VENUS

*B*rilliant star, requiring not the darkness of
the night to shine that others are dependent on,
for only darkness grants them visibility.
Star, with your orbit ended, you disappear

when other stars begin their celestial course
through the slow descending darkness of the night.
Glorious star, protector of love's priestesses,
your light kindled by your own incandescence,

till at last, transfigured, but never dimming,
you sink far to the West where sank the sun:
surpassing a thousandfold your ascendance
with the dazzling light of your descent.

DEATH

*C*ome thou, thou last one, whom I recognize,
unbearable pain throughout this body's fabric:
as I in my spirit burned, see, I now burn in thee:
the wood that long resisted the advancing flames
which thou kept flaring, I now am nourishing
and burn in thee.

My gentle and mild being through thy ruthless fury
has turned into a raging hell that is not from here.
Quite pure, quite free of future planning, I mounted
the tangled funeral pyre built for my suffering,
so sure of nothing more to buy for future needs,
while in my heart the stored reserves kept silent.

Is it still I, who there past all recognition burn?
Memories I do not seize and bring inside.
O life!   O living!   O to be outside!
And I in flames. And no one here who knows me.

*This poem - written in mid-December 1926 - is the last entry in
Rilke's note book, less than two weeks before the poet's death at
the age of 51.*

*It is ironic that Rilke's death resulted from a cut by a thorn as he
was gathering some of his beloved roses at Muzot castle.*

THE ROSE'S INNERNESS

*W*here is to this innerness
an outwardness? Upon what ache
do you lay its soothing petals?
What heavens find their reflections
in the secluded sea
of these wide open roses,
these carefree floating blossoms, see:
how loosely they lie in their looseness,
as if a trembling hand
could never spill and so disperse them.
They barely manage to stay afloat;
many of them let themselves
be filled to overflowing
and now flow over with inner space
into the days that ever more fully
encircle them, until the whole of summer
is contained in one room,
a room envisioned in a dream.

EPITAPH

*R*ose, o pure contradiction,
desire to be no one's sleep
under so many eyelids.

(Rose, oh reiner Widerspruch,
Lust, niemandes Schlaf zu sein
unter soviel Lidern.)

*Rilke prepared this epitaph for
himself in October 1925.
It is inscribed on his tombstone in
the churchyard of Raron parish,
Switzerland.*

1875   December 4: René Maria Rilke born in Prague.
Parents: Josef Rilke and Sophie (Phia) née Entz.

1885   Rilke's parents are separated.

1886   Rilke enters the Junior Military Academy in St.
Pölten.

1890   Enters the Senior Military Academy at
Mährisch-Weisskirchen, ending same in 1891 and
enrolling in business school in Linz.

1892   Returns to Prague; begins private study for his
diploma.

1894   Publishes first poems: *Life and Songs.*

1895   Receives his diploma. Enrolls in the University of
Prague for the winter semester: art history, philosophy, literature.

1896   Moves to Munich. Attends art history courses at
University. Writes for various periodicals. Meets
Wassermann. Has more early poems published.

1897   First meeting with Lou Andreas-Salomé; Gerhart
Hauptmann. Continues studies in Berlin. Publishes *Traumgekrönt.* His drama *Im Frühfrost* is
performed in Prague. Visits Italy.

1899   In Vienna meets Schnitzler, von Hofmannsthal.
At Easter returns to Berlin and begins his first
journey to Russia as guest of the Andreas-Salomé's. Meeting with Tolstoy.

1900   Second journey to Russia with Lou Andreas-Salomé. Visits Tolstoy in Jasnaja Poljana; visits to
Moscow, St. Petersburg.

After his return meets his future wife, Clara

Westhoff, and her friend, the painter Paula Becker. His *Stories of God* are published.

1901 He marries the sculptor Clara Westhoff. Birth of daughter Ruth.

1903 The third part of *Das Stundenbuch* is completed and the book published. He visits Rodin in Paris, is accepted as his private secretary and begins work on his monograph on Rodin.

1904 Visits to Rome, Copenhagen, Sweden. Second edition of *Stories of God.*

1905 He visits Rodin at Meudon, and undertakes his first lecture tour reading from *The Book of Hours (Das Stundenbuch).*

1906 Paris. Second lecture tour. Death of his father in Prague. *The Book of Images (Das Buch der Bilder),* begun in 1902, now completed and printed. Final version of *The Cornet* published.

1907 Third lecture tour. Vienna. Venice. The first part of *New Poems (Neue Gedichte)* published. *Auguste Rodin* monograph extended in a new edition.

1908 The second part of the *New Poems* is published; as is his translation of the Elizabeth Barrett-Browning *Sonnets from the Portuguese.* Meeting with Gide.

1909 Meets Princess Marie von Thurn und Taxis Hohenlohe. *Requiem, Early Poems* published. Journeys to Paris and Provence.

1910 Visits with his publisher, Kippenberg, and with the Princess Taxis at her castles in Duino and Lautschin, Bohemia. Returns to Paris. North-

African jouney: Algiers, Tunis. The *Notebook of Malte Laurids Brigge* is published.

1911   Naples, Egypt, journey on the Nile to Asswan. Back to Paris. Winter of 1911/12 at Duino Castle.

1912   The first Elegies written at Duino. In Venice meets Eleonora Duse. Munich, Paris. Journey to Spain: winter 1912/13 in Toledo and Ronda, Toledo, Cordoba and Seville.

1913   Stays in Ronda from January to mid-February. *Das Marienleben* (*The Life of the Virgin Mary*) published.

1914   On the move: Paris, Berlin, Munich, Zurich, Duino Castle, Venice, Assisi, Milan, back to Paris, return to Munich, Leipzig, Frankfurt, Würzburg; and end of the year in Berlin.

1915   Stays initially in Munich; to Berlin at end of year; then on to Vienna.

1916   Military Service in and around Vienna. From end of July Munich. Work in the war archives. Visits Zweig, Kassner.

1917/18/19   Residence: Munich. Visits with Count Kessler.

1919   Until mid-June: Munich. Mid-June to end of September in Switzerland: Bern, Nyon, Geneva, Zurich, Soglio, Lausanne. End of November lectures in Basel, Bern, Winterthur. Meeting with the brothers Reinhart, Nanny Wunderly-Volkart, Genf.

1920   Locarno, Basel. Reunion with Princess Marie von Thurn und Taxis Hohenlohe in Venice. Meeting with Baladine Klossowska, former friend from Paris.

1921 Berg: Meeting with Paul Valéry. From Sierre: discovery of Chateau de Muzot, where he resides from end of July on.

1922 Residence: Muzot. Daughter Ruth marries Dr. Carl Sieber. In February completion of the *Duino Elegies* and the *Sonnets to Orpheus*. Visitors: Princess Taxis, publisher Kippenberg.

1923 Muzot. Journeys in Switzerland. The *Duino Elegies* and the *Sonnets to Orpheus* are published. Rilke begins work on translating Valéry's poetry.

1924 Valmont: First visit to the clinic and hospitalization. First poems written in French. Visitors: wife Clara, Valéry, Princess Marie. Bad Ragaz, Lausanne, Valmont.

1925 Paris: from January till August. Then Valmont, Bern, Muzot. Rilke writes his will and last testament. Celebrates his 50th. birthday alone at Chateau Muzot. Translates Valéry poems

1926 In the Valmont Sanatorium till June. Meeting with Valéry. His book of French poems entitled *Vergers* is published on November 30. Rilke dies of leukemia at Valmont Sanatorium on December 29. He was buried as he wished to be in the churchyard of the village of Raron on January 2, 1927.